S0-BXW-794

Handbook for
Today's Catholic Family

Foundations – Prayers – Resources

A Redemptorist Pastoral Publication

St. Louis de Montfort
11441 Hague Rd.
Fishers, IN 46038

LIGUORI
PUBLICATIONS

One Liguori Drive
Liguori, Mo. 63057
(314) 464-2500

Imprimi Potest:
Edmund T. Langton, C.SS.R.
Provincial, St. Louis Province
Redemptorist Fathers

Imprimatur:
+ John N. Wurm, S.T.D., Ph.D.
Vicar General, Archdiocese of St. Louis

Copyright © 1979, Liguori Publications
ISBN 0-89243-112-1
Printed in U.S.A.

Grateful acknowledgment is made for use of excerpts
from:
   Ecclesiam Suam, by Pope Paul VI, Copyright ©
1964, by Paulist Press.
   A Reader in Natural Family Planning, published by
the Human Life Center, St. John's University, Col-
legeville, MN 56321. Copyright © 1978.
   The Bible text in this publication is from the Revised
Standard Version Bible, Catholic Edition, copyrighted
© 1965 and 1966 by the Division of Christian
Education of the National Council of the Churches of
Christ in the U.S.A., and used by permission.

Contents

SECTION TWO: CATHOLIC FAMILY PRAYERS

SECTION THREE: CATHOLIC FAMILY RESOURCES

Introduction

In Krakow, a rabbi dreamt three times that an angel told him to go to Livovna. "In front of the palace there, near a bridge," the angel said, "you will learn where a treasure is hidden."

The rabbi went to Livovna. When he arrived at the palace, he found a sentinel near the bridge, so he told him the dream. The sentinel replied: "I, too, have had a dream. The angel told me to go to a rabbi's house in Krakow, where a treasure is buried in front of the fireplace." Hearing this, the rabbi returned home and dug in front of his fireplace. There he found the treasure.

As a *family,* you have a treasure that surpasses all human expectations. That treasure is waiting to be discovered in your own home.

As *Catholic,* you possess a family treasure that can transform your life together into an experience of peace and joy. That treasure is waiting to be discovered in your own home.

You are the rabbi, and this booklet is the sentinel. The sentinel's message is this: *The kingdom of God is in the midst of you.*

SECTION ONE: CATHOLIC FAMILY FOUNDATIONS

1

You Are Called to Discover the Kingdom

The Secret of Adulthood

Wordsworth once wrote:

Heaven lies about us in our infancy;
Shades of the prison house begin to close
   Upon the growing boy;
But he beholds the light, and whence it flows
   He sees it in his joy.
The youth who daily farther from the East
Must travel, still is nature's priest,
   And by the vision splendid
   Is on his way attended.
At length the man perceives it die away
And fade into the light of common day.

The fading of "the vision splendid" into the light of common day is a loss that many adults experience. In his book *How to Meditate,* psychologist Lawrence LeShan speaks of it as "something of ourselves we once dimly and unknowingly had and have lost, without knowing what it was or where or how we lost it."

Many adults feel the loss. Once we enter the world of adult and family responsibility, life becomes work, work, work. It is a rat race we do not especially like but cannot put a stop to. Life becomes the joyless burden of Adam and Eve banished from Paradise.

Paradise was when we were little children. Though we had childish cares, life for most of us was an almost carefree existence, a dwelling in the fantasy land of eternal now. As we entered school age, we developed the desire to "grow up." But even the adulthood we envisioned was a fantasy. We figured we would become nurses or pilots and live happily ever after.

Now we are here in adulthood, the long middle stage between first and second childhood. Few of us are nurses or pilots. We are working away at raising a family, fighting inflation, coping with change, and looking for peace of mind.

Peace of mind and a sense of joy are what many of us really seek. We want to *experience* life and take pleasure in simple things. We want to break down artificial barriers and be ourselves. We want to be real with each other. We want, deep down, to believe that life is unbelievably good, and that it never ends. We want to remain responsible adults, but we want to live life with the "vision splendid" that our children and grandchildren possess.

Is there a way to regain that vision?

The Vision Regained

In his first letter to Corinth, Paul wrote, "When I became a man I gave up childish ways." Paul was addressing a group of adults who were trying to upstage each other by claiming they had various spiritual gifts (read chapters 12 through 14 of 1 Corinthians). These Christians were so busy with their petty scheming and rivalries that they had lost sight of their original vision. They had fallen into the trap of playing games with each other — a characteristic of the "adult" world. What Paul was telling them is that all this adult game-playing is really "childish."

Opposed to "childish" is the radically mature vision that Jesus revealed. He said: *Change and become like little children* (Matthew 18:3).

This strange advice sounds really foolish. And by our adult standards it is. That is the point. The vision that is offered to us

8

cuts through all the adult foolishness that makes us unhappy. Very simply, in Paul's words, *the foolishness of God is wiser than men* (1 Cor 1:25).

God's foolishness knows what adult wisdom does not know: that we cannot *make* ourselves happy. What the wise child in us wants is attainable — but we can attain it only by entering the world of Gospel simplicity. Kitaro Nishida, a philosopher, once wrote in his diary: "If my heart can become pure and simple like that of a child, I think there probably can be no greater happiness than this." We can become like that. We can experience what Saint Paul called "the glorious freedom of the children of God" (Romans 8:21).

The proposal is utterly serious: Change. Become like little children. Study the attitudes that set them apart from the world of adult wisdom. Pick a little child you know whose life embodies the view of life you want to regain. You certainly know such a child. In fact, she or he may very well live with you.

Study the child. Write down a brief list of her or his characteristics — things like *Trust, Wonder, Innocence, Joy.* Get inside the child's mind and explore where these attitudes come from. Ask yourself why he or she feels this way. Ask yourself whether he or she is foolish, or whether this is the way life really is — the way it can be for you.

Little children know what Jesus means by "blessed" in chapter 5 of Matthew. They know what Paul means by "joy" in his letter to the Philippians. In the world of little children, life is unbelievably good, and never ends. That world is exactly what Jesus was talking about when he spoke of the kingdom.

That world can be your world. You can see your own life in a new light. You can experience "the vision splendid" within your own home. But to regain that vision, you must take Jesus with utter seriousness. He was speaking to adults when he said: *Change and become like little children.*

The Family of the Kingdom

Jesus of Nazareth, the traveling preacher, had no property, no children, no steady job. You might not think such a person would be a great "family man." But he was exactly that. The difference was this — to him *everybody* was family who wanted to belong.

It all stemmed from the way Jesus saw reality. To him, home was the presence of God. He was aware of God the way you are aware of yourself — always and everywhere. In those days it was considered irreverent even to speak the name of God in public. The name was too sacred. But Jesus went much further than saying "God"; he called God *Abba* — Beloved Father. His relationship with God was so deep and natural that it was catching. Everyone he influenced was drawn into it. Even today people still talk to God in Jesus' daring terms; we call God "our Father."

Jesus was a rabbi, a religious teacher. But because of the way he saw reality, he was not like other rabbis. Jesus' awareness was that the Father is preparing a great banquet for us in his kingdom. The strange thing about this banquet is its time and place. The time of the banquet is *now*. Jesus was constantly telling people that the banquet has already begun. And the place for the banquet is not somewhere else. It is *right here*. Jesus insisted that "the kingdom of God is in the midst of you." This awareness was so deep and radical that even today people still do not grasp it very well. The banquet in the kingdom is here and now? What does this mean?

John the Baptizer was a contemporary of Jesus, a visionary holy man if ever there was one. John was incredibly strict on himself. His clothing was made of camel hair and his food was locusts and wild honey. John told people that the kingdom is at hand and urged them to repent.

Jesus said something similar, but his awareness of God was vastly different from John's. In Jesus' awareness the banquet had already begun; this was no time for strict fasting. So Jesus made the rounds eating and drinking with all kinds of people, respectable or otherwise. The contrast between Jesus and John was so sharp that a saying about it appears in the Gospel: "For John came neither eating nor drinking, and they say 'He has a demon'; the Son of man came eating and drinking, and they say, 'Behold a glutton and a drunkard . . .' " (Matthew 11:18-19). Jesus was not a glutton or a drunkard, but he was very serious about the banquet. The time is now, he would say. The kingdom is in our midst and the banquet has already begun.

The Kingdom Here and Now

No one can tell us what the banquet really is. It cannot be explained, it can only be discovered. But we do know this: God is involved in it. God is Beloved Father, and you are his beloved family. *Your family* is God's family. Every person in your family, respectable or otherwise, has a place in the kingdom.

No one can define the kingdom. It has no boundaries of time or place. But this much is known: for you, it is here and now in your family. The nature of the kingdom is such that you experience it through others — especially those who mean the most to you. For you, the banquet takes place in your family or it does not take place at all.

The kingdom is not something you can make happen. Only God can do that. It lies in your future with God. The kingdom appears in your midst to lead you forward into that future. You and your family are pilgrims, traveling to a kingdom that is not of this world.

The banquet you are called to is not literally a meal. As Paul wrote, "the kingdom of God does not mean food and drink but righteousness and peace and joy in the Holy Spirit" (Romans 14:17). You cannot create this peace and joy. But you can discover it and experience it in your spouse, your parents, your children, your brothers and sisters. Whenever you make each other happy, the peace and joy of the banquet are a reality you actually experience. Whenever you forgive each other or do something to heal a wound, God is at work within you. When you look at each other and realize that the Father is calling this person to communion with himself, the kingdom is in your midst.

The person who called us to the kingdom is very family-minded. To him, his Father means everything. Bringing people together to experience the peace and joy of the Holy Spirit was the whole point of his life. His family is everybody who wants to belong to it and his invitation to the banquet is especially for *you*. You must believe that. Otherwise, it does not mean much to say: *The kingdom of God is in the midst of you* (Luke 17:21).

Points for Reflection and Dialogue

The points for reflection and dialogue you find here, and in the chapters that follow, are the most important words printed in this booklet. Their importance is that you and your family can use them to become closer and happier, more Christian, more Catholic.

● You cannot become all these things just by reading a book. But you can get a good start by *writing your own book*. So use these questions to write a book! It might take you weeks, even months, to write your book. But if you make a commitment to the project and follow it to the end, you will have created a family treasure.

● Make this a *family* book. Have everyone who can write answer the questions on paper. (Children who cannot write can draw. Some may want to write *and* draw.) After writing and drawing, share your answers. Take turns talking. Listen carefully. Never argue, but enter into each one's feelings and experiences. Set out to enjoy; do everything to make each time as enjoyable as possible. Eat and drink together: the kingdom of God is in the midst of you.

One way to schedule the project is to take a chapter at a time.

If you do it that way, you will want to write answers to only four or five of the questions. Another way is to stay with the same chapter over two or three sessions until you have covered all the questions. However you go about it, it is a good idea to have at least one family session a week.

• Some of the questions you find here will not be for everyone. The chapters to the married, for example, are beyond the experience of children. As a family, use only the questions everyone can relate to. Simplify questions for younger members. Make up your own questions.

• Save all the papers you write and draw on. Collect them, date them, and put them into a special family scrapbook. If you ever write this book a second time, you will want to see your writings from the first time. If you never rewrite this book, those pages you once wrote will be an heirloom that reveals your hearts and souls to your children's children.

1. The most beautiful memory I have from my early childhood is the time that . . . (Describe it as fully as possible.)
2. On that occasion I felt . . . (Describe as fully as possible how you felt.)
3. When I was five or so years old, what I wanted to be when I grew up was . . . (Describe what you *liked* about what you wanted to be.)
4. To me, peace of mind means . . . (Describe it as fully as possible.)
5. The most childish thing most adults seem to do is . . . (Tell why.)
6. The most kingdom-like quality each member of our family possesses is . . . (Write each person's name and personal quality.)
7. The person I am studying in this family has these qualities I want for my own . . . (Don't name the person, just the qualities.)

8. The person, place, or situation that reminds me most of God is . . . (Describe just what it is that gives you this impression.)
9. When I think of Jesus calling God *Abba,* Beloved Father, here is what I think he thought and felt . . . (Describe it as fully as possible.)
10. The most enjoyable meal I have ever experienced with our family was the time . . . (Describe what happened, and how you felt.)
11. When people would sit with Jesus, eating and drinking and listening to him, I think they must have thought and felt . . .
12. The thing about our family that means the most to me is . . . (Describe how you feel, and how different your life would be without this reality.)
13. The last time I experienced the peace and joy of God's kingdom here at home was when . . . (Describe what happened and how you felt about it.)
14. When I stop and think that the Father is calling each member of this family to communion with himself, I feel . . .
15. When I stop and think that the kingdom of God is right here in our family, I realize that . . .
16. The most "childish" thing we do that keeps our family from enjoying each other is . . .
17. The most "adult" thing we do that helps our family to enjoy each other is . . .

2

You Are Called to Be the Body of Jesus Christ

Saint Paul's Damascus Experience

An event that has profoundly shaped your view of life is recorded in chapters 9, 22, and 26 of Acts of the Apostles. It says there that a man named Saul of Tarsus was heading north on the road from Jerusalem to Damascus. His mission was to capture some members of the Way, a strange offshoot of Judaism that worshiped a dead Jew named Jesus of Nazareth. As Saul neared Damascus, all was well. Then, suddenly, there was a flash of light and Saul found himself on the ground, hearing a voice:

"Saul, Saul, why do you persecute me?"

Saul said: "Who are you, Lord?"

The voice said: *"I am Jesus, whom you are persecuting. . . ."*

Blinded by the experience, Saul was led by the hand into Damascus to the home of a member of the Way. For three days he sat there blind, touching neither food nor drink. He then was approached by a man named Ananias who laid his hands on Saul's head. Immediately Saul was filled with the Holy Spirit, and something like scales fell from his eyes. He could see. Saul was then baptized on the spot. After that he ate some food and started regaining his strength.

The rest is history. Saul went on to preach, write, travel, do time in countless jails, survive countless beatings. By the end of his life Saul had spread the Way throughout the Near East.

All that Paul ever said or did as an apostle flowed from that one experience. During three days of blindness, and for the rest of his life, that voice echoed in his mind: *"I am Jesus, whom you are persecuting. . . ."* These people he had captured and imprisoned — in some way, they were *Jesus.* That was the staggering truth contained in the revelation, *"Why do you persecute me . . . me . . . ME?"*

But that was not all. If Jesus was somehow one with his followers, it meant that he was not dead but alive — alive in them, and everywhere else. He could break into a person's life anytime, anywhere — for example, on a dirt road outside Damascus. He lives. HE LIVES!

You, Too, Are Called to Damascus

In 1964, a year after his election to the papacy, Pope Paul VI wrote an encyclical letter entitled *Ecclesiam Suam.* In that letter the Pope quoted the fifth-century words of Saint Augustine, who was echoing the Damascus experience of Paul: "Let us rejoice and give thanks that we have become not only Christians but Christ . . . *we have become Christ.* For if He is the Head, we are the members; He and we are the complete man. . . ."

This echo cuts through all the sound and fury arising from change in the Church of the 20th century. It takes us past the surface to the very heart of Christianity: *Jesus lives . . . we are his body . . . the time to rejoice is now.*

This echo calls you to change any attitude you may have standing between you and your body. For example:

Do you have any unpleasant memories of the Church in the past keeping you away from the Church in the present? If you do, consider this: Jesus lives *now* in his body. The Church is now, not in the past.

Do you let teachings or rules or practices in the Church keep you unduly from loving the Church itself? If you do, consider this: *we* — not things and practices — are the body of Jesus. To be a whole body, we need you. Don't let *things* keep you from *us*.

Do you have any feelings against anyone that keep you from living an active life in the body of Jesus? If you do, consider this: that person is not the whole Christ. Do your best to reconcile with that person, but do not reject the body of Christ because of one member.

Your whole family deserves to receive all the faith in the living Christ you can give to them. Don't hold back.

Your children deserve to receive a strong, practical example of lived Christianity they can carry into adulthood. Don't shortchange them.

Your fellow parishioners, though they may not say so, need the influence of your caring presence among them. Don't weaken the body of Jesus by withholding the vitality only you can put into it.

You yourself deserve to be more fully Catholic. And Catholics whom you know can bring you closer to the living Christ. The closer you are to this body, the closer you are to him. These people Saul persecuted are Jesus. These people Paul loved are the body in whom Jesus LIVES.

We are Saul, and we are Paul. We can persecute our own body, or we can love it. If we choose to stand back from it out of disgust or resentment, let us face clearly what we are doing. If we choose to love this body and to heal it, let us realize whom we are loving.

Your Own Family Is the Body of Christ

In its document on revelation, the Second Vatican Council stated that Church tradition *develops*, that "there is a *growth* in the understanding of the realities and the words which have been handed down . . ." (8).

A good case of such growth is Vatican II's own insight into family: "The family is, so to speak, the domestic Church" (*The Church*, 11).

After Vatican II Pope Paul VI returned again and again to this point of "the family as Church" in speeches he gave. In his 1975 letter on evangelization, Pope Paul wrote the following: ". . . the family has well deserved the beautiful name of 'domestic Church.' This means that *there should be found in every Christian family the various aspects of the entire Church*" (71).

That ray of light puts your family in a whole new perspective. It says, for example:

— The Church is the visible Body of Jesus Christ. As Church, *your family* is the visible Body of Jesus Christ.

— The Church is called to be the "universal sacrament of salvation," communicating the mystery of God's love for the human race. As Church, *your family* has this calling — to reveal God's incredible love inside your family and out.

Your Family as Church

With this new development in Church tradition, the nature of Christianity itself has become more clear. Just when you may have settled into thinking that "Church" meant bishops, priests, and religious, the word comes through that "Church" means your family. It is not that the clergy are trying to give you some of their workload because there are not enough priests to go around. No, your family *always* was Church. You *always* had this calling to live with such undisguised joy that people would say, "I want to belong to that. Look how they love one another."

The Church is a Family, and your flesh-and-blood family is Church. Your family isn't perfect. But then, when was the Church ever perfect? Your family has problems. But do they match the problems of the people in Paul's first letter to Corinth whom he calls "the saints"? How "perfect" you are as a family is beside the point. The point is:

— You are trying to help each other believe the Good News, despite the fact that it is so good it's hard to believe.

— You are trying to see Jesus in each other.

— You dare to talk to God as *Abba*, the Father who has made your family *his* family.

— You are trying to realize more and more that your family is *his* Body; that whatever happens to one of you happens to *him*.

Your oneness with Jesus is rooted in your Baptism, a reality that takes you into the heart of mystery. For example, "Do you not know that all of us who have been baptized into Christ Jesus were baptized into his *death*?" (Romans 6:3) This oneness you share with his death through Baptism makes you one with him in his new, unending *life*. Baptism also makes you "all one" in him (Galatians 3:28). This reality deserves to be celebrated — which is something you can do on the anniversary of each family member's Baptism. This basic oneness is also something to keep very clearly in mind if any of your family members are baptized Christians but not members of the Catholic Church.

In some mysterious way your family is one with Jesus. Through your family he *lives* and invites people to the coming banquet. He is doing it through you, and he will keep doing it until finally one day — as Saint Augustine wrote — "there will be one Christ, loving himself."

Points for Reflection and Dialogue

1. **When I think of Saul sitting blind for three days with "I am Jesus . . ." echoing in his mind, some of the things I think he must have said to God are . . .**

2. **When I think of the fact that Jesus is really LIVING, the main thought that comes to me is . . .**

3. **When I try to understand what Saint Augustine meant when he said "we have become Christ," the main thing that occurs to me is . . .**

4. **The most unpleasant memory I have of the Church in the past is . . .**

5. The thing I like most about the Church today is . . .

6. The thing I find hardest to live with in today's Church is . . .

7. My dream for the Catholic Church, which I love, is . . .

8. The one thing I personally plan to do to make that dream a reality is . . .

9. The main way I can help our family to realize what great faith we already have is . . .

10. The one Catholic I know who helps me more than anyone else to be closer to God is . . .

11. When I realize that to love or hurt my fellow Catholics is to love or hurt Jesus' body and Jesus himself, I want to . . .

12. The thing that seems strange about saying that *our family* is the body of Jesus is . . .

13. When I think that *our family* is called to reveal God's love at home and to other people, the main thought that comes to me is . . .

14. We want to deepen our family oneness in Jesus by celebrating the anniversaries of our Baptism. The dates on which we were baptized are . . .

15. When I think that whatever happens to any member of our family happens to Jesus, the feeling I have is . . .

16. To me, "our family is the domestic Church" means . . .

3

Spouses Are Called to Listen and Dialogue

Communication Is the Heart of Marriage

In *Fiddler on the Roof*, Tevye the Milkman is married to Golde. Their older children are now leaving home, one by one. Alone with Golde, Tevye springs the question: *"Do you love me?"* Caught off guard, Golde recites the hard life she has shared with him and says, "If that's not love, what is?" "Then you love me?" he asks. "I suppose I do," she answers. Then together they sing:

It doesn't change a thing, but even so . . .
After twenty-five years, it's nice to know.

It *is* nice to know. But it's more than just nice, for the words "I love you" hide even more than they reveal. If you can say those words to your spouse, you can reach back where they came from and reveal much more. And what you find yourself revealing can stop you in your tracks. Using various approaches, many thousands of couples have actually done this. They have dipped into their consciousness, past all the memories, and have come up with deep, personal feelings they hardly suspected were alive in their hearts. For example:

"It's funny how you can live with someone for so many years and not realize how much you love them. I love you so much I can't believe it."

"I've always been so independent and work-oriented, but what I've really wanted all these years is your love."

"I never realized how much you mean to me. If you died I don't know how I could go on living."

21

These are not words made up by songwriters. They are the deep-down realizations of middle-aged and older couples. They are the real thing.

This kind of communication is the heart of your marriage, because it gives you an experience of oneness that draws you even closer. It is an act of love that creates deeper love.

Verbal communication means talking on the same wavelength, being tuned in to each other. It is more than conversation, more than discussion. It is the opposite of debate, which tries to drive home points and win. It is your listening to each other, really paying attention to each other's here-and-now feelings even more than to the words. It is your revealing of self to each other, especially your deep sense of oneness with each other.

In even the closest of marriages, negative feelings crop up between spouses. Given the complexity of personalities and the strains under which people live, this is inevitable. For example, if both of you have been coping with chaos at opposite ends of town, it is not easy to tune in to each other when you meet at the end of the day. Many couples cope with negative feelings by fighting and then lapsing into silence. Others shut each other out from the start by going into a trance with a newspaper, television, or some form of work. The way to avoid such noncommunication is to *choose firmly and deliberately to communicate.* Verbal communication, or dialogue, cuts through negative feelings. Dialogue is the answer to feeling apart from each other.

Pope Paul's Guidelines for Dialogue

The guidelines for dialogue that Pope Paul VI offered in his encyclical letter *Ecclesiam Suam* fit many situations, including dialogue between spouses. Speaking of the method, the Pope said that its characteristics are:

1. Be Clear

"Clearness above all; the dialogue supposes and demands comprehensibility" (83). An important point in this regard is preparation. You cannot abruptly say "Let's talk" and expect instant dialogue. If you want to get down to real sharing, pick your time — a time when everything will be calm and quiet. Agree on the time beforehand. If you "spring" a dialogue on your partner and launch into something delicate, you are inviting tongue-tied confusion. Give each other time to ask: "Why do I want to talk?" If you want to talk in order to discuss or persuade, that is one thing. If you want to talk in order to get on the same wavelength and deepen your sense of oneness, that is something else. If you want to dialogue, take aim. Aim to express yourself clearly and specifically, avoiding general-statement words like "always" and "never." Aim to listen and experience each other as clearly as possible.

2. Be Gentle

"A second characteristic of the dialogue is its meekness, the virtue which Christ sets before us to be learned from Him: 'Learn from me, for I am meek and humble of heart' (Matt. 11, 29). The dialogue is not proud, it is not bitter, it is not offensive" (83). Sometimes your feelings may urge you to "come out fighting." Don't do it. If you have a complaint with some third party, don't take it out on your spouse. If you have a complaint with your spouse, that is a different case; your instinct then is to *change* your spouse's attitude and behavior. But fighting never brings about a real change in attitude. You cannot browbeat anyone into your own image and likeness. The key is humble love. Its power is such that it can do what fighting cannot do: change *both* of you.

Another case is the one in which disdain or arrogance takes the fore. You're "listening" and you think to yourself, "I've heard that story a hundred times." You have heard it before so you tune out, and there goes your dialogue. Try gentleness. The person you love is trying to express something personal you may never have *really* heard 100 times previously. Listen gently; it helps you hear what you usually block out.

3. Be Trusting

"Trust, not only in the power of one's words, but also in an attitude of welcoming the trust of the interlocutor. Trust promotes confidence and friendship. It binds hearts in mutual adherence to the good which excludes all self-seeking" (83). Trust — this is the crux. You have to trust *yourself* — trust that the self you reveal is even more lovable than you are now loved. You have to trust enough to reveal the *real* you — not the self you think you would like to be or the self you think your spouse would like you to be.

You have to trust your *spouse* — trust that he or she is ready to accept you with real understanding. You have to trust like an innocent child who *knows* she is loved, like an infant who is perfectly confident that he will not be dropped or injured.

You have to *let go;* stop clinging to that part of you that fears hurt and rejection; put yourself, vulnerable, in your spouse's hands.

Lack of trust is like an invisible wall. As long as it is there between you, you can see each other but cannot make real contact. You help each other to lower the wall by saying "I love you" and revealing the deep feelings that are packed into those words.

4. Be Prudent

"Finally . . . prudence strives to learn the sensitivities of the hearer and requires that we adapt ourselves and the manner of our presentation in a reasonable way lest we be displeasing and incomprehensible to him" (84). Dialogue becomes unfruitful if negative feelings are allowed to take control. Good dialogue calls for good judgment. If you *know* or *suspect* that saying this or that will hurt your spouse, *don't say it.*

It can be helpful to reveal a negative feeling about something that happened today involving your spouse. But make sure you express just that: *your feeling*. If you shift the focus away from your feeling to the other person, the person feels accused or attacked. For example, it can be helpful to say something like, "I felt frustrated and discouraged when you didn't call me at five o'clock." But it never helps to say: "Why didn't you call me at five o'clock like we agreed?" Once you criticize, the invisible wall goes up and contact is lost. Put the emphasis on *your feeling*, not on what your spouse said or did.

When it comes to good memories, go back as far as you want. But leave bad memories alone. Do not go back past yesterday when it comes to anything unpleasant that took place between you. (There are therapeutic processes that focus on bad memories. The dialogue described here is something else entirely.) The focus of dialogue is you and me, here and now: how I feel about myself, you, and us at this moment. If you maintain this focus, with the attitudes recommended by Pope Paul, your dialogue will be rewarding.

Before Speaking, Listen

Later on in *Ecclesiam Suam*, Pope Paul makes an observation about dialogue that deserves special emphasis. He says: "*Before speaking, it is necessary to listen, not only to a man's voice, but to his heart*" (90). Heart — that is the heart of true dialogue. Listening means being conscious of a *person*, feelings as well as words.

In order to listen to the total person, you need total attention. You have to clear your mind of past and future — what happened an hour ago, what you are going to do an hour from now.

"*Before speaking . . . listen.*" Be careful that you are not thinking of what you want to say next instead of paying attention to what your spouse is saying now.

Pay attention to everything about your spouse. *Look* at him or her. Be physically close to heighten your sense of presence — not half a room apart, or across the table from each other. Notice your spouse's eyes and facial expressions; they can reveal as much as words can. Notice your spouse's body position, and hands and feet.

Pay attention especially to your spouse's tone of voice. Words tell you ideas; the tone of voice lets you in on a whole world of feeling. Feelings are like a window on the person's inner world. Your spouse's tone of voice can reveal that world to you. On the surface, words can be telling you a set of ideas. But on a deeper level, your spouse's voice can be telling you much more.

Listening is anything but a passive experience. It takes concentration to focus on a person. This total attention is a message in itself. It tells your spouse: "I really care about you. I'm trying. I want to receive everything you want to give me at this moment." This message closes the gap between persons and helps the person speaking to trust and reveal. Listening is an act of love that creates relationship.

Further Suggestions for Dialogue

The suggestions offered above pertain to all serious verbal communication between you and your spouse. But dialogue, as some couples practice it, is a special activity in its own right. Couples who "dialogue" set aside certain times for it and go about it in a certain way.

Some couples dialogue every day, others less often. If you take up the practice — and you can only gain by doing so — you need to schedule it. If you dialogue only when you feel like it, you soon end up not doing it. "More important things" always win out when there is no commitment to it. It is either "every evening at 7" or "Sundays at noon" or it is not at all. Few couples would disagree with the idea of spending two hours a week in dialogue. After all, there are 168 hours in a week; one

26

eighty-fourth of that time is not much to devote to something as important as your relationship. But very few couples spend even a half hour a week deliberately trying to communicate. It comes down to real priorities. You can say that your priorities are such-and-such. But does the way you spend your time match your theory?

Method and Topics

Many couples have found that writing is their key to fruitful dialogue. They begin by writing each other a letter. They pick a topic and write for 10 minutes, telling how they feel about each other and about their relationship. After writing, they read what each other has written. Then, for another 10 minutes, they share those same thoughts and feelings out loud. This "love letter" approach has a number of benefits. One benefit is that it makes for clearness, which Pope Paul recommended. For a couple who are just beginning to dialogue, writing helps to "break the ice." It makes it easier to express sentiments you might otherwise feel hesitant or embarrassed to express. Couples who tend to "write off" this writing approach without ever trying it never experience what they deprive themselves of. Couples who have made a commitment to this practice possess notebooks containing words every spouse needs and wants to hear.

Regarding topics for dialogue, things you share in common are always a good choice. Some couples formulate their topics in the form of questions about feelings. For example: "How do I feel when you pay me a compliment? (*Or:* when you get upset with me? when you are "up"? when you are "down"?) This area — how we influence each other's feelings — is uncharted territory for many couples. (For more on feelings, read "A List of Feeling Words," following this section.)

Almost anything about your life can be the focus of dialogue. But some areas are deeper than others. If you have become used to sharing in this way, you can get into areas most couples never venture into, such as *possessions; sex; death; God*. It is easy to look at those words on a page. But revealing your personal feelings about them to each other — that takes courage and trust. Try it and see.

As a couple, you have the awesome power to deepen each other's ability to love and to accept love. This deepening takes place when you truly communicate. You release God's creative love, allowing you and then others to experience the banquet that has already begun. *The kingdom of God is in the midst of you*. That is most evident when you are in dialogue.

A List of Feeling Words

The kind of dialogue recommended here embodies the wisdom of Jesus, expressed in Matthew 7:1 — "Judge not." But avoiding judgments in personal dialogue is not easy. One way to avoid them is to leave unsaid any sentence in which the word *that* would follow "I feel." For example, "I feel *that* it's too early" expresses a judgment, not a feeling. "I feel *comfortable (sad, confused, relaxed)*" expresses a feeling. When you write or say "I feel" in dialogue, follow it with a feeling word.

You can use the list of feeling words given here to begin a list of your own. Add other words that express other feelings you sometimes experience.

Affectionate	Beaten	Calm	Contemptuous
Afraid	Belligerent	Carefree	Contented
Aggressive	Bewildered	Cautious	Cooperative
Airy	Bored	Choked up	Courageous
Alarmed	Breathless	Close	
Angry	Burdened	Comforted	Dead-eyed
Anxious	Bushed	Compassionate	Deferential
Appealing		Confident	Defiant
Ashamed		Confused	Dependent

28

Depressed
Determined
Dishonest
Distant
Dominant
Dull

Ecstatic
Edgy
Embarrassed
Empathetic
Enraged
Envious
Estranged
Evasive
Excited

Fearful
Firm
Frisky
Frustrated

Giddy
Grateful
Grief-stricken
Grumpy

Guilty
Gutless

Happy
Hard
Hopeful
Hopeless
Horrified
Humble

Immobilized
Impatient
Inadequate
Independent
Insecure
Irritated
Itchy

Jealous
Joyful

Light
Locked in
Lonely
Loving

Mixed up

Nauseated

Open

Panicky
Paralyzed
Peaceful
Played out
Pleased
Powerless
Proud

Quiet

Relaxed
Resentful
Respectful

Sad
Scared
Seductive
Self-assured
Sexy
Silly
Soft
Spineless

Stretched
Strong
Submissive
Sunshiny
Surprised
Sweaty
Sympathetic

Talkative
Taut
Tender
Tense
Terrified
Thankful
Threatened
Thrilled
Timid
Tolerant
Torn
Two-faced

Uptight

Vacant

Warm
Weepy

Points for Reflection and Dialogue

This chapter is for the couple. Please go through the dialogue points together — because that is how you really experience what this chapter is about. One of the main reasons some couples are not closer is that they do not realize how close they actually are. This is a chance for you to realize that, and to deepen your married love.

As in the other chapters, do not take all of the points here at one time. The best way is to take one point a day on consecutive days, writing and then reading each other's answer and then talking. Pick a time and a place, and try it. If you have never done this kind of thing before, be ready for a surprise. Once you take the plunge, you will understand much better what "the kingdom in your midst" can mean to you.

1. **When I think back on all you have done for me, the one thing that stands out in my mind is . . . (Tell what it is and the feeling this memory brings. Write for at least five minutes, not more than ten.)**
2. **When I think that some couples go 25 or more years loving each other without really expressing it in a way that lights up their lives, I want to say to you . . .**
3. **When I say "I love you," part of what I mean is . . .**
4. **When I talk to you and I sense that you are really trying to understand me, the feeling I have about you is . . .**
5. **When I think of the fact that you love me just as I am, the feelings I have about myself and about you are . . .**
6. **When you look into my eyes, the feeling that comes to me is . . .**
7. **When you are trying to tell me how you feel, and I realize I am failing you by talking about "facts" or "the way things are objectively," the feelings I have about myself and about you are . . .**
8. **Though I know you better than anybody else, there is so much about you I don't know. The most recent thing that helped me to realize this was . . .**
9. **When we are going through our wedding album like this, the main feeling that comes to me is . . . (If you want, select your favorite pictures and write about them one at a time, a day at a time.)**
10. **When I look at this present you gave me before we were married, the memory and feeling it revives are . . .**

11. When we play "our song" like we just did (or we hear it played), the memory and feeling it revives are . . . (If you want, pick several favorite songs and write about them one at a time, a day at a time.)

12. When you accepted the little gift I just bought (or made) for you, my feeling about you was . . .

13. When I received this little gift you just bought (or made) for me, my feeling about you was . . .

14. Someone wrote: To say "I love you" is to say "You will never die." What this means to me about you is . . .

4

Spouses Are Called to Married Intimacy

The Intimate Garden

In the Book of Genesis, the story of Adam and Eve takes place in a garden setting. Estranged from God and from the garden he gave them, the man and the woman now have only each other. Whatever garden they experience from now on must come from their life together.

Most husbands and wives can appreciate the story. The world you live in is hardly a garden. Having become "one flesh," you toil together not only for bread but for happiness. You have each other, and you know deep down that the only real garden in your lives is the one you live in together. The years come and go. Children come into your lives, then leave for gardens of their own. What is left is the core of your world: God and each other, and finally . . . God.

Your garden of intimacy is the heart of your life together, and at the center of that garden is your experience of being "one flesh." The value of that experience cannot be overstated, because when it is an expression of personal love, it creates deeper love. As Vatican II stated it, "This love is uniquely expressed and perfected through the marital act" (*Church in the Modern World*, 49).

Communication Is the Secret

Your sexual life together can deepen your personal intimacy. But you deepen personal intimacy through sex only when your sexual expression communicates personal intimacy that is already there. If sex is impersonal, it does not deepen a marriage.

There are two secrets to making sex an expression of personal intimacy. The first secret is to keep in mind that *everything else* about your relationship as a couple influences your sexual communication. One thing this means is that the waking hours before sexual communication need to be a time of *personal* communication. If they are not that, then there is need — before sex — for personal dialogue. Closeness begets closeness. Noncommunication begets no sex, impersonal sex, or sex that does not communicate all the underlying love you really have for each other.

The second secret regards the time right before, during, and after sexual love. The secret is to express yourself in ways your spouse understands and appreciates. The secret is to try to share yourself with all the trust and tenderness you have at a given moment. The secret is to strive for the same qualities of gentleness, trust, prudence, and attention to each other that make for true dialogue. The heart of the secret, in fact, is actual dialogue. Without loving verbal communication, your bodily communication lacks the fullness of personal intimacy it could have. When it comes to the human, spiritual, sacramental depths of sexual love, personal communication can make all the difference.

Sexual Myths and Real Problems

Sexuality is a deep part of the human mystery — so deep that every civilization has used sexual images and myths to express the mystery. But there are also some very shallow sexual myths. When people buy the shallow myths, sex is dehumanized and personal relationships are destroyed.

One shallow myth about sex is that you should "perform" — and achieve sexual "success" — by following certain patterns. It simply is not necessary to have trim, youthful bodies and to perform like superstars in order to experience deep, abiding sexual intimacy. There is no need to compare your personal situation to that of others or to the standards made up by the latest sex oracles. The wiser guides in the matter urge against that. Genuine guides, such as Dr. James J. Rue, Ph.D., counsel that each husband and wife is unique when it comes to sexual needs and satisfactions. No one pattern of sexual activity applies to all husbands and wives.

This means that it is not a good idea to compare your sexual patterns to those of other couples. It means that there is no scorecard to keep regarding frequency of sex — how many times per week or month. It means that there is no timeclock for how long foreplay should last. It means that there are no rules of order for bodily positions, or for what times of day or night sex should take place. Sex is a personal expression, and every couple is unique. Unless there is freedom from made-up goals, quotas, and expectations, sex cannot be an expression of personal intimacy.

Another myth about sex is that it is simply a means to my own private satisfaction. Pleasure is an integral part of sexual satisfaction, but the pleasure of sex is paradoxical. Seek pleasure as pleasure and it is fleeting. Seek pleasure to express love, to achieve deeper oneness, and it satisfies in a way that is abiding.

In your intimate garden, you are "one flesh," one body. Your sexual intimacy — a basic expression of Matrimony, your personal sacrament — sustains and deepens your family oneness in Jesus Christ.

Sexual Problems Need Communication

It is not uncommon for husbands and wives to experience physical problems related to sex. Two common problems experienced by some men, for example, are secondary impotence (inability to sustain an erection sufficient for penetration), and premature ejaculation. Two common problems experienced by some women are frigidity and nonorgasm.

These problems can have various causes. Stress or declining health, for example, can cause secondary impotence. Fear of failing to perform well, or the husband's lack of sensitivity, can cause frigidity or nonorgasm. In such problems there is almost always this common thread: the problem in one way or another originates with *both* spouses. Likewise, the solution to the problem rests with both spouses. A sure way to prolong or aggravate such problems is to ignore them; to carry unexpressed bad feelings about them; to express resentment or hostility. What is needed and called for is dialogue — open, trust-filled communication. This is no time to fight or bury feelings; it is a time for love. Without personal intimacy in such instances, there will be no physical intimacy.

It is also a time for common sense and humility. This may mean consulting a doctor — for example, in the case of poor health. Or it may mean consulting a counselor — for example, in the case of premature ejaculation where spouses need help to synchronize their activity. Getting help in such cases amounts to an act of love for Christ and his body, because a problem in the area of physical intimacy can affect personal intimacy — and that affects us all.

Good News for Intimacy: Natural Family Planning

In the late 1960s, millions of adult Catholics read *Humanae Vitae,* the 1968 encyclical letter of Pope Paul VI which rejected artificial forms of birth control. Since that time, theologians and scientists have made immense progress toward the positive "integral vision of man and of his vocation" put forth in the encylical. A major contribution to that vision are the scientific advances in natural family planning (NFP).

Around the world there is a ground swell of interest in NFP on the part of young women who fear the Pill and other artificial means of birth control. Disenchantment with artificial means coincides with the spread of research-perfected NFP, which is safe, reliable, harmless, and costs absolutely nothing. In 1979 Father Anthony Zimmerman, executive director of the Family Life Association of Tokyo, wrote: "We are on the eve, I believe, of a major watershed in human history, when a major part of the human race is about to turn to natural family planning as a means of improving family life. Once its practice is diffused among the race, it will probably be continued until the end of time."

More Than Another "Method"

NFP is much more than a natural answer to artificial birth control. One of the most striking values people experience from it is that it improves their family life. As they check the monthly cycle and make decisions together, couples report a whole new dimension in their communication as spouses. A heightening of communication and sexual interest go together. Couples who have switched from artificial means commonly remark as follows. From wives: "Now my husband asks me again, and doesn't take me for granted any more." From husbands: "My wife is interested again; she reacts now like when we were first married."

A surprise to many is that NFP makes people more aware of the kingdom of God in their midst. A statement signed by a number of missionaries from the Far East and South America said that NFP brought about the following results: "Family life has improved greatly . . . . Parents are giving more attention to the Christian education of their children and to family prayer . . . . People have more confidence in their priest, realizing that he is concerned with their problems and can speak about things that were once taboo . . . . Non-Christians have come into the Church."

Natural family planning is almost too good to be true. But there is no need to take it on faith; places to write and call for information and contacts are listed in the "Catholic Family Resources" section of this booklet.

The intimate garden you share as spouses is the place where you experience the kingdom of peace and joy in the Spirit. It is from this experience of "one flesh" that your married love goes out and gives life to the rest of Christ's body, beginning with your own family.

Points for Reflection and Dialogue

This chapter is another good opportunity to deepen your personal closeness. It can also help you to renew your sexual communication. So take the opportunity. Discover new areas of intimacy in your garden by doing these questions together one by one.

1. When I think of us as "two in one flesh," working our way through life together, I think . . .
2. When I think of our marriage as an intimate garden that nobody lives in but you, me, and God, I realize . . .
3. When I think of our garden together as "the core of our world," my thoughts are . . .
4. The activity in our daily life together that helps me to feel closest to you is . . .
5. The quality you show that does the most to make our lovemaking an experience of love is . . . (Describe how this quality influences your attitude and feelings.)
6. The way I want to trust you more when we are making love is . . .
7. One way you can help me to communicate better when we are making love is . . .
8. The last time we made love, what we talked about beforehand was . . .
9. The last time we made love, what we talked about afterwards was . . .
10. What I would like to talk about beforehand to make our sexual communication more personal is . . .

11. What I would like to talk about afterward to make our lovemaking experience more personal is . . .
12. What I have heard or read until now about natural family planning, and my reaction to it, is . . .
13. The reason we want to look into natural family planning to get an accurate, detailed picture of it is because . . .
14. The place(s) listed in the "Catholic Family Resources" section of this booklet that we have decided to write (or phone) for information about natural family planning is (are) . . .
15. The way you put me first in your life that I most appreciate is . . .
16. When I realize that you and I can always love each other more and more if we really want to, I . . .
17. When I think that our personal intimacy can give others a consciousness of Christ's loving presence in their lives, I . . .

5

You Are Called to Listen and Pray Together

Listening through Sacred Scripture

In *The Heart Is a Lonely Hunter,* Mr. Singer is a deaf-mute of great sensitivity. He can't speak or hear, but he has a "listening heart." In the story, a bum who has no other friends tells Mr. Singer: "You're the only person who ever listened to me." Mr. Singer's caring raises people out of their loneliness. But none of his friends sense that he, too, needs "listening." Sadly, in the end, he escapes his pain by taking his own life. Only then, at his grave, does a young friend say: "I loved you, Mr. Singer."

You live with people who need your listening heart. And you live with God, whose deep desire is that you listen to *his* heart. Here and now, God calls to you through the words of sacred Scripture. In the words of Vatican II, he invites you "through the fullness of his love . . . into his own company." His great desire is that you listen to him in Scripture and respond to him in prayer. As Vatican II urged, "prayer should accompany the reading of sacred Scripture" (*Revelation,* 2 and 25).

Suggestions for Family Scripture

Up until Vatican II, reading and praying Scripture was a tradition of relatively few Catholic families. If your family has not made that experience a regular part of your life together, take the following suggestions and see how they fit your circumstances. If Scripture is already part of your family tradition, these suggestions may contain a few helpful ideas for you, too.

• Read and pray Scripture together regularly. How often and how long varies with each family. Choose your times, then be faithful to them.

For families with younger members, the children's bedtime can be a good time for a brief reading of a favorite Gospel passage. Before the main meal of the day is a time other families may find better. After the reading, your meal prayer together can be based on what the Lord has communicated to you through the Scripture.

A longer session at least once a week is also a good idea. For many, Saturday or Sunday evening is an ideal time. Once you have chosen the time that is best, consider it sacred — a time when you deliberately want to be together to love one another by sharing the Word.

• Let the children do as much as possible; active involvement is the key to maintaining their interest. Every contribution they make should be appreciated, no matter how young they are. Do your best to make these get-togethers a joyful experience for the children. In later life, their memories of these times will have a profound influence on their relationships with you, with each other, and with God.

• When you meet to read and pray, have two dictionaries on hand: a regular one and a Bible dictionary. One of the most useful and inexpensive Bible dictionaries is *The New World Dictionary-Concordance to the New American Bible*. (This book is published in a paperback edition by World Publishing, 2080 W. 117th Street, Cleveland, OH 44111.) When you come to a word you are not sure of, look it up in a dictionary.

You will also want a Bible atlas for maps. *Atlas of the Bible Lands* is a good one. (This book is published in a paperback edition by Hammond, Inc., Maplewood, NJ 07040.) Some Bibles include good maps; check to see whether yours does.

• Memorize favorite Scripture passages. For children, this practice will result in a valuable treasure when they reach adulthood. It is also a treasure for adult memories now. You can make this practice really enjoyable if you hold family contests and give little prizes.

• Prayer should be a part of every family meeting with Scripture. After reading and sharing your thoughts, give each family member a chance simply to talk to Jesus or the Father or the Spirit. (If you are reading Saint Paul or one of the prophets, talk to them too; they hear you.) Take turns talking in your own words. If the Spirit moves the group to pray in silence, that too is very good. Parents, during this prayer time, remember to express your own personal response to God, avoiding sermonettes aimed at the children.

A Format for Family Scripture

A simple format you can use for Scripture together is the following:

1. Everyone focus on the presence of Jesus in your midst. "Where two or three are gathered in my name, there am I in the midst of them" (Matthew 18:20).

2. A family member reads the chosen passage. Whoever is reading this time gets to choose the passage (unless you are taking one book of the Bible and following it through).

3. After the reading, begin to digest it. Here are two among many ways to do this. These two approaches can be used separately, or they can be combined.

— A study-oriented approach is to take the passage chosen and to understand it in connection with the chapter or section it is a part of. The headings in *The Jerusalem Bible* and *The New American Bible* are helpful in this regard. Use all available commentary: the footnotes on the page, and the introduction (when there is one) at the beginnings of the Gospel, letter, or book. Also use your dictionaries and Bible atlas. Try to get the general sense of the passage as a whole, as well as the meaning of the individual sentences.

— A more personal approach is the following. All reflect on the passage just read for a minute or two. Then, for about five minutes, all write (or draw) the thoughts and feelings that came to them from the reading. (This can be a letter to the Father, the Son, or the Spirit, like the "dialogue letter" described in chapter 3.) A focus question you can use to write your response to most readings is: *What did the Lord tell me in this reading that can make us a closer family?*

4. Share together. Take turns telling or reading what each person wrote or drew or learned from research. After all have had their turn, invite general remarks about what was said and specific suggestions for the future. Perhaps a family resolution — something *positive* that all can do between now and next time — can be made.

5. If there is any other activity — a memorization contest, a Scripture game, or a snack — this is a good time for it.

6. Pray together, as recommended above.

7. Share a sign of peace and joy: embrace, shake hands, kiss. Take your time; talk to each other personally. Express love, forgiveness, joy in being together. The kingdom of God is in the midst of you!

Listening through Silent Prayer

Family prayer takes many forms. Various methods or techniques, such as the rosary, can be used together as well as privately. One thing to remember about any prayer technique, old or new, is that it is good for you if it helps you to be in touch with God — and not good for you if it does not.

In connection with techniques or methods, there is also this to remember about prayer: *all* prayer is supernatural in the sense that it is a response to God that begins with a grace from God. If your prayer is real, it is supernatural prayer regardless of the technique you use. (For a fuller appreciation of this point, consult the writings of Father Basil Pennington listed in the "Catholic Family Resources" section.)

Two methods of silent prayer are offered here. In each case, you can use the method privately and keep it private — or you can make it part of family prayer.

Alphonsian Meditation

The first method, a simple meditation technique designed by Saint Alphonsus Liguori, is as follows:

1. *Preparation.* As a remote preparation, try to stay conscious of God as you go about your daily schedule. Remind yourself frequently of this truth: God is here; I am in his presence like a fish is in the water. God is loving Father, and I am his loving son or daughter.

To start the meditation, focus on God's presence with an act of faith. Ask his pardon for any faults you recall. Ask for help to make a good meditation. Add a prayer to our Blessed Mother and other favorite saints for help.

2. *Consideration.* After reading for a few minutes from sacred Scripture (or some other spiritual book), ask yourself: What have I read? What does it say to me? What have I done about this up until now? What shall I do about it in the future?

The advantage of meditation is not so much in thinking about things as in the prayer that this leads to. So devote the greater part of meditation to affections (short prayers from the heart), petitions (requests for help from God), and resolutions (practical plans for changing your life, with God's help).

Affections: "Lord, I am sorry for having offended you." — "Thank you for the blessings you have given me." — "I want to love you above all things." — "I praise you, Lord!" — "I place my trust in you."

Petitions: Ask for whatever you need — for example, forgiveness of sins, greater confidence, help in a stressful situation, grace to forgive someone, to be more patient, to die a good death.

Resolutions: Make them short and specific — for example, to stop gossiping with . . . to be kind to . . . not to lose patience with . . . .

3. *Conclusion.* (a) Thank God for the insights and graces gained during this meditation; (b) repeat your resolutions; (c) ask for help to keep your resolutions; (d) choose a thought or short prayer to carry with you during the rest of the day.

Centering Prayer

The second method is called centering prayer, a term inspired by the Trappist monk and writer Thomas Merton. Centering prayer, as offered here, is a simplified form of the prayer found in the 14th-century Catholic spiritual classic, *The Cloud of Unknowing.* (For further reference to this book, see the "Catholic Family Resources" section.) The method is as follows:

1. Find a quiet place, sit in a comfortable position, and close your eyes. Relax all your muscles as completely as possible. Relax your mind and enjoy the inner calm.

2. For several moments focus calmly on God — Father, Son, and Spirit — at the center of your being. God is the Center who is everywhere, and present at the deep center of your soul. Focus on that center and allow yourself to experience God present within it.

3. Let a word come to you — a simple word like *God, Father, Love, Jesus, Lord,* or *Yahweh.* Slowly and calmly repeat the word. Let it lead you into God present at your center. Focus all your attention and desire on God, and *let your word express all the faith, hope, love, and praise within you.* If any thoughts or imaginings cause you to lose your focus, simply return to the center by repeating your word.

4. When you are ending your prayer, do it slowly and calmly. Slowly repeat a prayer such as the Our Father, the Hail Mary, or the Glory Be to the Father, experiencing all that the words bring to you.

Further Points on Silent Prayer

If you use either meditation or centering prayer privately, the usual length of time for the prayer is about 20 minutes at least once (if possible, twice) a day. If you use either of these methods as a family practice, you may want to shorten the time to less than 20 minutes. Both of these simple methods can be used by younger children, but the length of time should be adjusted to their capacity. In shortened form, these prayer methods can be used at the time for silent prayer in your family Scripture get-togethers.

If you make silent prayer a part of your Scripture together, experiment not only with the length of time for it but also with the spot it occupies. For example, you may want to have silent prayer right after the Scripture reading. One benefit of this arrangement is that in the sharing which comes next, you can all listen to what each person has experienced in silence with God.

In your relationship with God through Scripture and listening, there is what the eminent theologian Bernard Lonergan has called the "inner word" and the "outer word." The outer word is the meaning that comes to you from understanding Scripture itself. In and through the Scripture you read or hear, you may receive an "inner word" — the word God speaks to your heart. This is the word Jesus was talking about when he said: "Blessed are you, Simon Bar-Jona! For flesh and blood has not revealed this to you, but my Father who is in heaven" (Matthew 16:17).

Receiving this inner word is not something you can make happen. It is grace, an experience of the kingdom in your midst. But you can prepare for it by faithful listening. Hearing the inner word is something like hearing *through* the words a person is saying to what the person's heart is saying. It is from God's heart to yours.

The heart is a lonely hunter. As St. Augustine said so poignantly, *Our hearts are restless, Lord, until they rest in you.* When you listen to God and to each other with enough love, your hearts become full.

Points for Reflection and Dialogue

1. When I think God wants me, is inviting me, to be intimate with him, I . . .
2. The main reason I have not spent more time with sacred Scripture in the past is . . .
3. The reason I want to make Scripture a more regular part of my life is because . . .
4. The day and the time we agreed to read Scripture together is . . .
5. The Scripture passage we all like that we choose for our next Scripture reading is . . .
6. The favorite Scripture passage that each of us has chosen to memorize for next time is . . . (List each person's favorite passage.)
7. The main blessing I think we received from our last Scripture get-together was . . .
8. What I want to do at our next Scripture reading, to help our family to get more out of it, is . . .
9. The method of silent prayer that helps me most to be in touch with God is . . .
10. The length of time I find is best for my silent prayer is . . .
11. As a result of our family group experience with silent prayer, we . . .
12. The greatest gift I have received from listening to God in Scripture is . . .
13. The greatest gift I have received from listening to my family sharing their experience of God is . . .
14. As a result of our experience together, I now realize . . .
15. As a result of our experience together, I now resolve . . .

6

You Are Called to Family Forgiveness

A Way of Family Forgiveness

I am Jesus whom you are persecuting . . . persecuting . . . persecuting. Why do you persecute me . . . me . . . ME?

Those words echoed in the memory of Paul until the day he died. As the years went on, the meaning of those words became clearer and clearer to him, until Paul could declare: *If one member suffers, all suffer together; if one member is honored, all rejoice together* (1 Cor 12:26).

As a family with Jesus in your midst, you are called to reconcile when you cause each other suffering. You are called to use the power you have — the power to share his forgiveness. Coming together and being healed by that forgiveness is one of the most amazing graces you possess. The more you use this grace, the more you experience the presence and love of Christ in your family.

Focus on Family Relationships

The following few pages contain a list of positive and negative points, some of which you will recognize as part of your family life. The negative points (in the left-hand column) are ways in which you are capable of weakening your family body — ways of causing suffering and alienation. The positive elements (in the right-hand column) are ways in which you strengthen your family body — ways of deepening your closeness and joy.

This list can be used in various ways. You can use it just as it is, or (this may be a better idea) you can use it to *make up your own list* — one that contains more of the positive and negative things you experience together. You may want to have two lists: one for adults and teenagers, and a second, simpler one for younger members.

In using your list, be sure to keep a balance between positive and negative. If you used only the negative points, you might get the impression that you do not love your family very much. But that just is not true. The fact is that you are much more loving than unloving. If you find it easier to spot negative elements in your own conduct, this means mainly that you are not as loving toward *yourself* as you could be.

Go down both columns, and focus on your relationships in the family by writing (or thinking of) one person's name in each box you select. Be selective; zero in on the ones that apply to you, and skip the rest. One set of points might look like this:

SHARING *versus* SELFISHNESS	
I shared with . . .	**I was selfish to . . .**
John by being generous with my time.	_Ellen_ by being stingy with my time.

After coming together and centering on the presence of Jesus in your midst, pray for a spirit of love and forgiveness. Then, silently together, go down your list(s) point by point. At the end of the list you will find some suggestions on how to proceed after that.

SHARING *versus* SELFISHNESS	
I shared with . . .	**I was selfish to . . .**
_____ by being generous with my time.	_____ by being stingy with my time.
_____ by volunteering to help out.	_____ by avoiding a chance to help out.
_____ by being generous with my clothes, toys, equipment.	_____ by being selfish with my clothes, toys, equipment.
_____ by gladly doing it his/her way.	_____ by insisting that it be done *my* way.
_____ by saying, "Sure, I can spare the time."	_____ by saying, "Sorry, I haven't got the time."
_____ by saying, "Let's do it together."	_____ by saying, "It's *your* job, *your* turn."
_____ by saying, "Let's try it your way."	_____ by saying, "Don't do it that way."

CARING *versus* INDIFFERENCE	
I cared about . . .	**I was indifferent to . . .**
_____ by listening when . . .	_____ by not listening when . . .
_____ by asking him/her how he/she felt about . . .	_____ by not caring how he/she felt about . . .
_____ by taking him/her seriously about . . .	_____ by making fun of him/her.
_____ by asking . . .	_____ by demanding . . .

RESPECT *versus* DISRESPECT	
I respected . . .	**I was disrespectful to . . .**
_____ by caring whether I would hurt his/her feelings.	_____ by not caring whether I would hurt his/her feelings.
_____ by asking whether I hurt his/her feelings.	_____ by not caring whether I *did* hurt his/her feelings.
_____ by giving full attention to him/her when . . .	_____ by acting occupied when . . .
_____ by dropping what I was doing when . . .	_____ by complaining when . . .
_____ by . . .	_____ by . . .

PRAISE *versus* CRITICISM	
I praised . . .	**I criticized . . .**
_____ for doing . . .	_____ for doing . . .
_____ for remembering to . . .	_____ for forgetting to . . .
_____ for looking nice.	_____ for the way he/she looked.
_____ for the way he/she . . .	_____ for the way he/she . . .
_____ by saying, "Thanks for . . ."	_____ by saying, "It's about time."
_____ by saying, "You're good at . . ."	_____ by saying, "You never . . ."

_____ by saying something gentle when I was upset.	_____ by saying, "Shut up!"
_____ by calling him/her a nickname he/she likes.	_____ by calling him/her a name he/she doesn't like.
_____ by saying . . .	_____ by saying . . .
_____ by saying . . .	_____ by saying . . .

TRUST *versus* SUSPICION	
I trusted . . .	**I was suspicious of . . .**
_____ and showed it when . . .	_____ by thinking I couldn't trust him/her when . . .
_____ by trusting that he/she would tell me when . . .	_____ by trying to worm information out of him/her when . . .
_____ by thinking of a good reason he/she had for doing . . .	_____ by thinking he/she was trying to make me feel bad when . . .
_____ by taking his/her word for it when . . .	_____ by suspecting he/she lied to me when . . .
_____ by thinking, "Maybe the mistake was mine."	_____ by saying, "It's your fault."
_____ by presuming he/she was doing something good.	_____ by saying, "What are you doing now?"

UNDERSTANDING *versus* CONTROL	
I tried to understand . . .	**I tried to control . . .**
_____ by treating him/her the way I'd like to be treated when . . .	_____ by being bossy when . . .
_____ by realizing that he/she has feelings like I do.	_____ by making threats when . . .
_____ by realizing that he/she deserves my deepest respect.	_____ by nagging and picking at him/her.
_____ by letting him/her be when there is no harm in it.	_____ by saying "No" frequently.
_____ by laying conditions on him/her only when necessary.	_____ by saying, "unless," "or else."
_____ by being willing to go along with him/her when . . .	_____ by saying, "Why should I?"

MAKING PEACE *versus* FIGHTING	
I made peace with . . .	**I fought with . . .**
_____ by saying, "I love you."	_____ by teasing him/her.
_____ by saying, "Let's be friends and talk."	_____ by starting an argument with him/her.
_____ by refusing to push, shove, hit, or slap when . . .	_____ by pushing, shoving, hitting, or slapping him/her.

_____ by express-ing my *feeling* (see page 25).	_____ by deliber-ately doing something to annoy him/her.
_____ by asking forgiveness when . . .	_____ by accusing him/her of . . .
_____ by following my rule never to hurt a family member.	_____ by insulting him/her or being sarcastic.

FORGIVENESS *versus* HOSTILITY	
I was forgiving toward . . .	**I was hostile toward . . .**
_____ by sacrific-ing my pride and making the first move when . . .	_____ by main-taining a "cold war" with him/her when . . .
_____ by saying, "Let's be friends" when . . .	_____ by acting aloof when . . .
_____ by touching him/her gently when . . .	_____ by slamming the door or breaking something when . . .
_____ by saying sincerely, "That's OK; I know you didn't mean it" when . . .	_____ by getting upset with him/her when . . .
_____ by saying, "I'm really sorry; please forgive me" when . . .	_____ by refusing to approach him/her after I had hurt him/her by . . .
_____ by saying, "You're right; let's make up" when . . .	_____ by refusing to accept his/her attempt to reconcile with me when . . .

Once you have all gone through your lists, go back over the *positive* points you noted. Then *thank* God for the love you have been given. Be thankful, because this is evidence of his loving presence in your own being.

After thanking God, go back over the *negative* points you noted. Ask for forgiveness. And ask for help to ask forgiveness of someone whose name you noted after one of the negative points. In a moment you are going to go to *one* of your family members and ask forgiveness for *one* negative point.

All together (joining hands, if you want to), pray the Our Father. Now go to the person you are asking forgiveness of. Simply say something like: "Gerald, I was selfish with you when I told you I didn't have time to pick up your coat at the cleaner's. *Please forgive me.*" After that, embrace, shake hands, or give some other sign of friendship.

When someone asks forgiveness from you, say simply and sincerely: "I forgive you, Jennifer, and I love you."

If the person you want to approach is talking to another family member, ask someone else for forgiveness or join hands with the other person and quietly pray the Our Father together.

After all have asked and given forgiveness, join together again and say a final prayer. Then have one of the family singers lead a song that captures the spirit of the occasion.

Toward the Sacrament of Reconciliation

The method of family forgiveness outlined above can be done in a brief 10-minute get-together. It can also be part of a longer family Scripture or prayer session (see chapter 5).

Once you experience the good that can come from forgiving each other as a family, the thing to do is to agree on a schedule for future sessions. This planning ahead is very important. If you say, "Let's do this again some time," its chances of taking place are minimal. Be convinced that this kind of family love deserves real priority in your life together, and *build it into your schedule by marking it down on your calendar.*

At the least, you will want to schedule family forgiveness two times a year — before Christmas and Easter. These are special times for the sacrament of Penance. Regardless of how you confess to the priest (face-to-face or in a confessional), your spirit of contrition and love can be deepened immeasurably by having family forgiveness at home *before* you approach the sacrament. The grace of the sacrament depends on your personal attitudes of contrition, love of God, and purpose of amendment. There is no better way to kindle these attitudes than by experiencing the love of Christ in family forgiveness.

Family forgiveness is not the sacrament of Penance, and is in no way a substitute for it. But the two go together in a beautiful way. In family forgiveness you experience the love of Christ, the healing of his body, and your own family as Church. In the sacrament of Penance, you experience Christ's sure sign of forgiveness — absolution of your sins — and your deep oneness with the whole body of Catholics in whom he truly *lives*.

Points for Reflection and Dialogue

1. The words "I am Jesus . . . Why do you persecute ME?" are about my own family. When I let that truth sink in, I realize that . . .
2. "If one member suffers, all suffer together." What this means to me, when I think of my family, is . . .
3. The way in which I am most sharing in our family is . . .
4. The way in which I want to be more sharing is . . .
5. The way in which I am most caring in our family is . . .
6. The way in which I want to be more caring is . . .
7. The person in our family I tend to praise most is . . .
8. The person in our family I tend to criticize most is . . .
9. The way I am going to stop criticizing and start praising (name) is . . . (Make very specific plans that you intend to carry out starting now.)

10. The person in our family to whom I am most respectful is . . .
11. The way in which I am most disrespectful is . . .
12. The way I plan to deepen my love and respect for (name) is . . . (Make specific plans.)
13. The person in our family I am most trusting toward is . . .
14. The way in which I am most distrustful or suspicious is . . .
15. The way I plan to deepen our family closeness by being more trusting is . . .
16. The main way I tend to control things is by . . .
17. The way I plan to be more understanding toward (name) is by . . . (Make specific plans.)
18. The main way I take away from the peace of Christ in our family is by . . .
19. The way I intend to deepen the peace of Christ in our family is by . . .
20. The way I was hostile last time to a family member was . . .
21. The person I intend to ask forgiveness of is . . .
22. The way I plan to do it is . . .
23. The greatest gift I have received from experiencing family reconciliation is . . .
24. The schedule we have agreed to set for family forgiveness is . . . (Write down the various dates and times.)
25. The reason I want to prepare better for the sacrament of Penance is because . . .
26. The way in which I plan to make the sacrament of Penance more of a way of loving our family as Christ's body is . . . (Make specific plans.)

7

You Are Called to Family Eucharist

The Eucharist, Center of Family Life

A most fascinating yet basic symbol in nature is the mandala, a circular design that radiates outward from a point at the center. The flat top of a tree stump is a perfect mandala — rings growing outward from a central point of life. Nature produces mandalas, such as flowers opening out, in wild generosity. Artists use the design to express what words and even music cannot say.

The meanings found in the mandala are as varied as its forms. Through the ages it has symbolized wholeness, organic oneness, healing, and growth, all finding their source in the life-giving center. Dynamic life flows from the center, yet it is what T. S. Eliot in *Burnt Norton* called "the still point of the turning world."

For Catholics, the great mandala of Christian life always has been and always will be Jesus Christ in the Eucharist. He is, in the words of Pope John Paul II, "the center of the universe and of history." As Saint Paul discovered on the road outside Damascus, Christ is not limited by what we call time and space. His presence envelops and passes through the space-time continuum. And yet we can know him "in the breaking of the bread" (Luke 24:35). In that act of nourishment, we experience the living Center of our existence uniting us, his body, ever more closely to the source of Life that has no limits.

Center of Meaning

Your life is organized in all kinds of ways. And yet, despite all the programing of human life, you may know the feeling many people express — that their lives have no real center. All the activity, the competition, the getting ahead — it all seems to lead nowhere. At the deep level where we all really live, these people experience their center as a void, an empty place that sends this silent message: Your life is a senseless trip in a mindless universe, ending in oblivion.

There are many people who are not afflicted with that dis-ease. Among them are Catholics who have never lost, or who have recovered, the Center of their lives — that living Bread who nourishes his body with meaning and unity.

The key to your meaning and oneness as a family is to deepen or recover your Center. Every day you work, play, study, eat, sleep. This can be an endless round of mere functions, a series of meaningless movements. But it does not have to be that way. You can focus on the Center and let your life together flow toward and out from it. You can consciously let that Center tie together all the scattered remnants of your days into one meaningful reality of never-ending value. You can focus on the Eucharist with such steady consciousness that it becomes your "still point," the silent source of Life that lets your family realize the depth of Paul's words: *Because there is one bread, we who are many are one body, for we all partake of the one bread* (1 Cor 10:17).

Focus of Family Meals

At home, one of the most valuable ways of focusing on the Eucharist is to make it the Center of attention at the start of family meals. In some households, circumstances do not allow family meals to resemble the kingdom banquet of peace and joy. In other households family meals hardly ever take place. In these situations, patient, continuing dialogue is perhaps the best approach to realizing the great importance of breaking bread together.

But even in less-than-ideal circumstances, it is possible to lead off the meal with a moment of deep attention to Jesus Christ. This moment is part of the grace before the meal, but it needs to be a special moment — a brief silent time for each person to focus on the living Bread. Make this moment specifically Eucharistic: train your hearts on the Eucharist and realize your oneness with each other in him. If you each memorize the above words of 1 Corinthians 10:17 and repeat them in your heart before every family meal, the Eucharistic Presence will in time become the still point of your turning world.

Sunday Mass, Banquet of Family Oneness

The Eucharist is the living Center of Catholic life. But history shows how easy it is to lose vital contact with that Center. As early as the year A.D. 57, one group of Christians had let the Eucharistic gathering degenerate into a time of excessive drinking, alienation, and hurt feelings. In chapter 11 of 1 Corinthians, Paul brought that group back to reality by reminding them in no uncertain terms: This is Christ you are profaning!

Loss of contact with the Eucharist today takes different forms from the ones Paul encountered. But the solution is the same. You can experience deeper meaning and joy in Sunday Mass if you focus more deeply on Christ at the Center of it all. Once the basic insight comes into focus — that "Christ is all, and in all" (Col 3:11) — everything else falls into perspective. The following suggestions may help your family to grow together into this realization.

• A very essential awareness to bring to Sunday Mass is a sense of Jesus' Passion, Death, and Resurrection. The readings from Scripture each Sunday always show a different side of the mystery of Christ. Altogether, the readings for the various Sundays over a three-year period give a total picture. But at the very center of that picture is the unchanging core of what each Mass is all about: his Passion, Death, and Resurrection. When you focus on the different Sunday readings, it is essential not to lose sight of that vital Center.

Basing your family Scripture get-togethers (recommended in chapter 5) on the readings for Sunday Mass is an excellent way to link family Scripture with Sunday Eucharist. If your get-togethers are on Saturday evening or Sunday morning before Mass, they can be the perfect time to relive the key events of Last Supper and Passion-Death-Resurrection recorded in these 18 chapters: Matthew 26-28, Mark 14-16, Luke 22-24, and John 13-21. There is no need to make these chapters the main reading for your session; one or more of the Sunday readings can be the topic at the start of the session. But it is extremely valuable to have a thoughtful reading of *one* of the 18 key Gospel chapters just before your get-together breaks up. If you read one of these chapters each week at your Scripture session, you focus on each of them at least twice a year.

• If your family Scripture sessions are based on the Sunday readings, your attention to the readings and homily at Sunday Mass can be a fuller experience than it would otherwise be. As you listen to the readings, let memories of your family sharing come to mind; they bring out the family-Church dimension of the Word you are hearing. Do the same thing during the homily. Far from being a distraction to what the homily offers, your memories from family Scripture can help the homily to reinforce your sense of family oneness.

• At the Offertory of the Mass, consciously turn your mind to each member of your family. As a family, the main thing you offer to God in Jesus can be *your sense of family oneness*. You desire this oneness, and you work to discover the kingdom in your midst. Now is the time to offer your efforts and the graced experience of closeness that flow from those efforts. If you are right next to each other at the time, give each other a look of recognition to remind yourselves of what you are offering. (This alone is a key reason to be together as a family, whenever possible, at Sunday Mass.)

• During the Eucharistic Prayer (after the Preface up to the Lord's Prayer), focus on Jesus who is with you here and now, reenacting his Passion, Death, and Resurrection. Keep this focus, and let the words of the Eucharistic Prayer lend meaning to it. Let the memory of your last Gospel reading from one of the 18 chapters become part of this presence. When the priest says "Do this in memory of me," at the heart of the Eucharistic Prayer, let your memory of the Last Supper be as vivid as possible.

• At the Sign of Peace, let it be a moment of special meaning for you as a family. It doesn't have to be anything showy; a look and a touch can say a great deal. If you have any affectionate nicknames or words for each other, say them now. (One father of a family says, "The peace of Christ, my little elf," to his young daughter. The daughter will always remember it.) The Sign of Peace is a special time for spouses; the words "I love you" can be truly significant at this moment.

• Holy Communion possesses such meaning that the reality of it cannot be fathomed by the human mind. But it is very important to focus on the depth of Holy Communion, realizing as much of it as you can before you partake. One beautiful formula you can memorize and repeat to yourself as you prepare to receive is this 13th-century antiphon for Corpus Christi:

O holy banquet, in which Christ is received,
the memory of his passion is renewed,

the soul is filled with grace,
and there is given to us a pledge of future glory.

At the moment you receive Communion, you say "Amen." St. Augustine wrote that when the priest stands before you at Communion and says "The body of Christ," you reply "Amen," meaning: *Yes, we are.* "We" means the threefold body of Christ: his risen body, his body the Church, and his Eucharistic body. When you say "Amen," you are saying "Yes, *we* are the body of Christ."

At the moment you receive, also recall the words of Paul that you repeat silently to yourself before meals: *Because there is one bread, we who are many are one body, for we all partake of the one bread.*

Then begin praying acts of love: love for Christ within you, love for his body — especially your family — with whom you are now more one than ever before. At this moment of Eucharist, the mysterious reality of Jesus' death becomes present here and now. So does the future of your life together in the kingdom. The future banquet is now. With Jesus, you and your family are now, as Augustine said, "one Christ loving himself."

Points for Reflection and Dialogue

1. When I see the mandala in nature that means the most to me, it makes me think of . . .
2. The "still point" of my world is . . . (As far as possible, tell why.)
3. When I read the Emmaus story in Luke 24:13-35, what it tells me about the Eucharist is . . .
4. When I think of people whose lives have no real center, I feel . . .
5. When I think that I can deepen the center of my life by being more serious about the Eucharist, I . . .
6. When I realize that the Eucharist is meant to be the center of our family life, I . . .

7. Since I started repeating 1 Corinthians 10:17 silently before family meals, I am beginning to realize . . .

8. When I try to probe the meaning of "Christ is all, and in all," the main thought or feeling that comes to me is . . .

9. Since we began reading the 18 chapters from the Gospels at our family Scripture, the main benefit I have gotten at Sunday Mass is . . .

10. Since we began linking our family Scripture with the Sunday readings, the main benefit I have gotten from the readings and homily at Mass is . . .

11. The main realization that comes to me when I offer our family oneness at the Offertory on Sunday is . . .

12. What the Eucharistic Prayer at Sunday Mass has meant to me since I began to focus on it more deeply is . . .

13. What the Sign of Peace has come to mean to me as a family sign is . . .

14. Now that I have memorized the antiphon "O holy banquet . . ." and repeat it to myself before Communion, the meaning it holds for me is . . .

15. Now that I receive Holy Communion as the banquet of our family oneness, the thoughts and feelings I have about Communion are . . . (Write as much as you can on this point.)

8

You Are Called to Evangelization

Your Family Is Called to Evangelize

If you were a first-century Christian trying to "write an orderly account" of the movement sparked by Jesus of Nazareth, how would you organize your material? This was one of the literary problems that Luke the Evangelist had to work out.

Studying Luke's two-part masterpiece — his Gospel and Acts of the Apostles — we can trace his method. In the Gospel, Luke's narrative is cast in the form of a journey *toward* Jerusalem, where Jesus has an appointment with death and Resurrection (read chapters 9 through 18). Picking up the narrative after the Resurrection, Acts records the astounding growth of the Christian movement, journeying outward *from* Jerusalem to "the end of the earth" (1:8).

This image — a community growing outward from its Center, the risen Jesus — is Luke's inspired way of delivering his Gospel message to your family. His message is: *You are Jesus' witnesses to the world*. Your calling as a family is to *be his body* in such a way that people sense this vital fact: JESUS LIVES.

In the seventh chapter of Luke's Gospel, religious seekers come to Jesus asking, "Are you he who is to come, or shall we look for another?" As Church, your family is living this calling when religious seekers look at you and ask themselves, "Is this where he is?"

In his document *On Evangelization in the Modern World,* Pope Paul VI declared that your fidelity to this calling is your "deepest identity." Your oneness in love as a family is the "wordless witness," the "authentically Christian life," that leads people to raise "irresistible questions" about the Church and about Christ himself. As the Pope expressed it, "Through this wordless witness these Christians stir up irresistible questions in the hearts of those who see how they live: Why are they like this? Why do they live in this way? What or who is it that inspires them? Why are they in our midst? Such a witness is already a silent proclamation of the Good News and a very powerful and effective one" *(Ev* 21; see also 71, 14, 41).

Witness of Life and Word

The "authentically Christian life" the Pope refers to says yes to these three questions: "Do you really believe what you are proclaiming? Do you live what you believe? Do you really preach what you live?" *(Ev* 76) Regarding the third question, the Pope recommends what Saint Peter called "always having 'your answer ready for people who ask you the reason for the hope that you all have'" *(Ev* 22; see 1 Peter 3:15-16).

If it is to speak to a person's heart, this verbal witness has to be personal. As the Pope points out, "In the long run, is there any other way of handing on the Gospel than by transmitting to another person one's *personal experience of faith*?" *(Ev* 46)

Your first reaction to this silent-then-verbal witness may be: "No one is going to look at our family and say, 'There is something about you. Why are you like that?' We're just not the type." If that is your reaction, give your family a break: think more highly of yourselves. God does. As a family that reads and prays sacred Scripture, that experiences mutual forgiveness, and oneness through the Eucharist, you *are* the type of family that causes people to sense something special. And if someone asks you about it, the fullness of your Christian Catholic experience together is the deep well from which you "have your answer ready." Your closeness as a Catholic family is the "outer word" through which God can and will speak his "inner word" to people's hearts.

What Is at Stake

The crucial importance of your answering this call to evangelization cannot be overstated. Nothing less than the credibility of the Church itself is at stake. People, including Catholics, find the Church credible when Catholics reveal the love of Christ. On the other side of the coin, people — including Catholics — find the Church in-credible (that is, un-believable, unconvincing) when Catholics do not reveal the love of Christ. As a family, you are now influencing the human shape of Christ's body that everyone around you sees. When they see you, do they ask, "Is this where he is?" Or do they find you such an unlikely body of Christ that they "look for another"?

As the presence of "new religions" around the world makes clear, what is ultimately at stake is the credibility of Jesus himself. The Pope states that "unity among his followers is not only the proof that we are his but also the proof that he is sent by the Father. It is the test of the credibility of Christians and *of Christ himself*" (*Ev* 77). This is a reference to the Last Supper, when Jesus prays, "that they may all be one . . . in us, *so that the world may believe that thou hast sent me*" (John 17:21). The "they" Jesus prays for is your family. *His* credibility depends on *your* witness. How totally Jesus appeals to those around you depends on your oneness. As the Pope says, very simply, "It is a question of people's salvation" (*Ev* 5).

Evangelization Begins at Home

The question arises: How does a family become "authentically Christian" enough so that other people experience Jesus through that family?

The Pope's answer is: "The Church . . . begins by *being* evangelized" (*Ev* 15). You begin with yourselves, at home.

What you are called to look at here are your goals — the things that stand out as the real priorities in your life together. As Father Basil Pennington puts it, "To try to teach the

Christian gospel with its strong bias for the poor and its way of daily abnegation — 'If you would be my disciple, take up your cross daily . . . and come follow me' (Luke 9:23) — and still to be busy pursuing the same pleasures and immediate goals as the worldly materialist, is to condemn oneself to a fruitless ministry.''

The priority of the Gospel is given to us with perfect clarity. Speaking not of wealth and comfort, but of basics like food and clothing, Jesus states: ''Your Father well knows that you need them . . . set your heart first on his kingdom . . .'' (Luke 12:30-31).

The way to make the priorities of the Gospel your *personal* priorities is to *go to the Gospel*. The way to make these priorities *family* priorities is to go to the Gospel *together*. In other words, read and pray sacred Scripture as a family. Soak up all the vision and inspiration you find there, and do not back away from the self-giving the Gospel calls for by putting it down as ''nice but impractical.'' Communicate and share your religious experience together. Seek forgiveness, and forgive one another. Make the Eucharist the Center of your family life. And always remember for whom you are doing this: for Christ, for his body, for those around you — including family members — who inwardly seek him. Do it because you love.

Paradoxical Happiness

''It is pointless to try to witness for God until you have known him, until you find him wonderful,'' says Scripture scholar Marilyn Norquist in *How to Read and Pray the Gospels*. But when you have made the decision to live the Gospel, you do find God wonderful. Once you have let God in the door, you experience ''the glorious freedom of the children of God'' that Paul talks about, the ''peace and joy in the Holy Spirit'' that is the kingdom (Romans 8:21, 14:17). Mere words do not express this reality. But as Pope Paul points out, ''The Lord will delight in describing in many ways the happiness of belonging to this Kingdom (a paradoxical happiness which is made up of things that the world rejects) . . ." (*Ev* 8; here the Holy Father is referring to Matthew 5:3-12: the Beatitudes). What your family can look forward to is nothing less than a new life together.

Evangelization Calls for Parish Unity

What Catholics are engaged in today is the same movement announced by Luke the Evangelist. We are spreading "to the end of the earth" the News that Jesus lives.

In this movement your family has a central role. Speaking of you and of every Catholic family you know, the Pope said that the family that evangelizes itself is "a place where the Gospel is transmitted and from which the Gospel radiates . . . And such a family becomes the evangelizer of many other families, and of the neighborhood of which it forms part" (*Ev* 71).

But how can one individual family possibly communicate what Christ means in their lives to the ocean of humanity around them? Isn't this the impossible dream?

No, it is not the impossible dream. First, and most basically, what is going on here is "too deep for words." It is the work of God "who searches the hearts of men." The witness you give of living constantly in your Father's presence is no more than The Spirit's entrée into people's hearts. "When we cry, 'Abba! Father!' *it is the Spirit himself bearing witness* with our spirit that we are children of God . . ." (read Romans 8). For now, the outcome is his secret.

Secondly, you are Catholic. In the Faith, you belong to the family of Catholics around you. The witness you give is not of some merely private life with God; it is the witness of your *unity with your Catholic family*. Unless people can see very clearly that you are *one body* in love with your Catholic family, you are not giving the witness Jesus needs in order to be credible: "that they may be one . . . in us, *so that the world may believe* that thou hast sent me." You not only are not alone; your witness is in-credible unless people see it as flowing from your oneness with your Catholic faith family.

This means a number of things that add up to unity. Here are a few examples.

Striving for Unity

● There is always a need for deeper dialogue with your ordained priests. As one body, all the members of the Church share in the priesthood of Christ, the head. But "all the members do not have the same function" (Romans 12:4). Ordained priests are "marked with a special character" by which they "act in the person of Christ the Head" (Vatican II, *Priests* 2). One of the key ways of deepening unity in your parish is by appreciating your priests as people. For example, praise that is honest gives them a sense of worth as persons and as priests. Criticism, on the other hand, erodes their sense of joy and relationship with the people they want to serve. So focus on their qualities of dedication, faith, perseverance. Give them ample credit; they really deserve it.

● One of the most valuable things you can do for vocations to the priesthood and religious life is to let your priests and religious feel appreciated. Those who know they are cherished by their people show it in their attitude. Perhaps more than anything else, it is their sense of belonging, of feeling at home in their vocation, that attracts young people to be like them. Vocations to priesthood and religious life come *to* individuals, but they come in large part *through* your day-to-day attitudes toward these persons in your parish. By affirming them today, you build the Church of tomorrow.

● In your family prayer, you can deepen your appreciation of your priests and religious by praying for each of them personally, not just as a group. You also deepen your sense of unity with the whole Church by praying for your local bishop and for the successor of Saint Peter, the Holy Father.

Awareness of unity with them is awareness of unity with the entire Church of today and of all times, past and future. Theological writer Gerald O'Collins has drawn attention to the fact that Saint Peter was the fundamental witness to the risen Jesus. As Peter's successor, the Pope is the fundamental witness that Jesus lives today. Our unity with the Pope's witness is one of our great bonds in the Faith.

Unity Among Parishioners

● You can strive for unity by seeking friendship with other Catholic families in the parish. In some places there are "family clusters" — groups of four or five families who share Scripture and prayer, recreate together, meet at the Eucharist, and cooperate in various forms of service to the community. In parishes where families form these Catholic clusters, without allowing them to become closed groups or merely social gatherings, parish unity can be immeasurably deepened.

In one metropolitan area, some 500 small groups of people were organized. As they focused on their faith in the light of the Gospel, these Catholics became more deeply aware of what the Faith they share means to them. The person who started these groups was the archbishop of Krakow, Cardinal Wojtyla, who became Pope John Paul II.

● A final example of striving for unity is self-examination that focuses on the quality of your parish life. You can do this at family Scripture gatherings, especially with the letters of Saint Paul. The Christian communities to which Paul wrote were not basically different from modern parishes. His first letter to Corinth, for example, could have been written to many a modern parish community. His letter to the Galatians provides a needed focus on faith and unity. His letter to Philippi, with its tone of joy and unity, is what every parish needs. Discover the principles and guidelines for unity that Paul formulates in these letters and check the quality of your parish life in light of them.

(An excellent booklet that combines suggestions for family Scripture with ways of deepening the unity of parish life is entitled *How to Read and Pray Saint Paul*. See the full reference to this work in "Catholic Family Resources.")

Animated by Love

"The work of evangelization," the Pope said, "presupposes in the evangelizer an ever increasing love for those whom he is evangelizing." This love has warmth; it possesses real affection and concern. The Pope describes it by quoting Saint Paul, saying: "With such yearning love we chose to impart to you not only the gospel of God but our very selves, so dear had you become to us" (1 Thes 2:8; *Ev* 79).

One way you can tell your love is real is if you have "respect for the religious and spiritual situation of those being evangelized. Respect for their tempo and pace . . . Respect for their conscience and convictions . . ." *(Ev* 79). The call to profound reverence for every person as "another self" stands out in the documents of Vatican II (see especially *Church in the Modern World*). In *Redeemer of Man*, his first encyclical letter, Pope John Paul II intensified the call with ringing words: "Respect each one's dignity and freedom!" (16) Respect for one another is so basic that without it there is no real evangelization.

Doing things for people — even religious things — is not a sure sign of love. Saint Paul makes this point in 1 Corinthians, 13:1-3. Unless our motive is selfless love, wrote Thomas Merton, we will communicate to people only "the contagion of our own obsessions, our aggressiveness, our egocentric ambitions, our delusions about ends and means, our doctrinaire prejudices and ideas." This is not only possible; it happens. Even in good works, "my" hidden (or not so hidden) obsessions and ambitions and prejudices can take over what ought to be the work of the Spirit. When this takes place, the result is disunity in the body of Christ.

One of the best safeguards against this counterfeit love is to look into the mirror of the Gospel. Ponder Matthew 25:31-46 to see whether it is really Christ you are loving. Dwell on 1 Corinthians 13:4-7 to see whether your love is genuine. Pray that you recognize Christ and love him — especially at home.

At the Service of All

Evangelization is a service to others that should be at the heart of every form of parish ministry. Offering the Gospel to people "with complete clarity and with a total respect for the free options which it presents" is the very work of God. People have a *right* to the Good News (*Ev* 80).

But works of "justice in charity" are also vitally important; without them evangelization is neither genuine nor credible (*Ev* 29-39). Ecumenism is another ministry that is vitally important, because the division among Christians "damages the most holy cause of preaching the Gospel to all men, and it impedes many from embracing the faith" (*Ev* 77). In parish ministry, however, evangelization can actually be undermined if there is no *family* witness. Without a commitment to family service to others, something vital is missing in your family and in your parish.

In your parish, neighborhood, city, there are family ministries that are simply waiting to be discovered. Who better than families, for example, can stand up to media propaganda that tears down the family? Letters signed by families say much more to an editor or a government official than does a letter from one individual. A family visiting the elderly communicates more joy than does a lone individual. This is only the beginning of a list of dozens of things you can do as a family. The witness of family is a powerful influence, even on the persons who are witnessing.

In seeking forms for your family ministry, join forces with other families. Two families can be better than one, and four can be better than two. Share your knowledge of the needs around you; even in affluent parishes the spiritual and corporal needs are enormous. Plan together. Pray together. Act together. And be a real part of the parish in your family ministry. Seek and welcome the cooperation and guidance of your priests and religious. In speaking of organized lay ministries, the Pope returns to the focus on unity: ''These ministries will have a real pastoral value to the extent that they are established with absolute respect for unity and adhering to the directives of the pastors, who are the ones responsible for the Church's unity and the builders thereof'' (*Ev* 73).

Centered in the Eucharist

Evangelization is like a liturgy of the Word that leads home to the Eucharist. But without a vigorous parish witness already *centered in the Eucharist,* we simply cannot evangelize in a way that *leads people home* to the Eucharist.

It is by renewing and deepening the Eucharistic unity of your parish that you deepen the credibility with which you carry the Good News ''to the end of the earth.''

• One key way to renew parish Eucharist, suggested in the previous chapter, is to make Sunday Mass a true celebration of *family* oneness. When you and the families around you at Mass do this, you will notice the difference.

• Another way to appreciate your parish oneness *during* Mass is to experience it *before* Mass. Arrive early, as if Mass starts 10 minutes before it actually does. Talk to people you know. Be especially on the lookout for people you do not know, and make it your family policy to welcome any new faces that appear. Get on a first-name basis with as many people as possible; they are all members of the Family.

• *During* the liturgy of the Eucharist, try to be keenly aware, whenever the priest raises the Host above the altar, that you are all one in that body of Jesus that is offered.

• At Communion time, after you have received his body and blood, set aside a special moment — half a minute or more — to dwell on the reality of your here-and-now oneness in Jesus with all these Family members who surround you.

• *After Mass,* stay around outside church. If possible, give your fellow parishioners at least 10 minutes. Make this your time for *them.* Think of this as an extension of your oneness in the Eucharist, for that is what it is. Think of them as your own relatives — because, in him, that is who they are. Invite people home for coffee. Talk about possibilities for service to needs in the parish. Invite other families, one by one, to your family Scripture get-togethers. Each Sunday, focus on the most positive experience you had during Mass and tell someone — at least a member of your own family — about it.

• There are countless other ways you can deepen the sense of Eucharist in your parish. Some people, for example, need a ride to church. Ask around for names; the priest is often a good source for such information. Not all — but some — people who do not often go to Mass would go if you invited them to accompany you. Be on the lookout for the right persons and the right moments.

• Go to Mass on weekdays whenever you can possibly make it. This alone can deepen your whole way of seeing yourself as a Catholic.

• If you work in a business area where there is a church with a noon Mass on weekdays, go to that Mass and take someone with you.

• If the children in your family have not had the experience of daily Mass, bring them into it. They have a right to it.

• Start a "daily Mass league" with other families in the parish who are committed to daily Mass. Encourage other families to make daily Mass a priority. (In some cases, this may entail deciding that morning Mass takes priority over late-night television.) Be a Catholic whose heart is drawn to that Center whose Presence is silent witness to the Love at the heart of this universe.

Points for Reflection and Dialogue

1. When I think of the sense of adventure the first Christians must have had in carrying the Good News "to the end of the earth," the feeling about evangelization I want to deepen is . . .
2. What I shared the last time I shared a "personal experience of faith" was . . .
3. The quality or pattern of life that is now our family's strongest witness to the Faith is . . .
4. The quality or pattern of life that we *want* as our family's strongest witness to the Faith is . . .
5. When I think that the credibility of Jesus himself depends on our family witness, the feelings and thoughts I have are . . .
6. In all honesty, the personal priorities that stand out when I look at my life are . . .
7. The Gospel priorities that I am most afraid of making my own are . . . (The reason for my fear, in each case, is . . .)
8. The Gospel priorities that I really want to begin making my own are . . .
9. The main way in which I am going to deepen my affirmation of our parish priests and religious in a regular way from now on is . . .
10. Three families we intend to approach about forming a "family cluster" are . . .
11. The letter of Saint Paul that we are going to read first, to deepen the quality of our parish life as a family, is . . .

12. The main person in our parish whom I have not reverenced as "another self" is . . .

13. What I must do first to allow God to strip away my egocenteredness is . . .

14. This is my personal list of things we can do together as a family in the service of others . . . (Write down three or four things that are practical for your family. Put everyone's written ideas together, then decide on the first thing you will actually do together. Keep the list for future use.)

15. The ways of deepening Eucharistic unity that we are going to begin doing this coming Sunday are . . .

16. Knowing that the Fathers of the early Church called the Eucharist "our daily bread," I want to go to Mass every day because . . .

17. The reason we try to go to Mass every day as a family is because . . .

18. "I am sure that neither death nor life . . . will be able to separate us from the love of God in Christ Jesus our Lord" (Romans 8:38-39). When I think of these words of Paul in connection with our family, I want to say . . . (Write as much as you can about this.)

SECTION TWO: CATHOLIC FAMILY PRAYERS

Introductory Note

Wholesome family traditions preserve and deepen family oneness. But a tradition of family prayer does much more: it deepens your conscious oneness *in Christ*. When you have developed a regular habit of praying together, you begin to sense a dimension of life that goes beyond the short span of earthly existence. In family prayer you can learn that the kingdom in your midst is the true home you are destined to share together always.

1. Sign of the Cross

In the name of the Father, and of the Son, and of the Holy Spirit, Amen. *(Said at the beginning and end of prayers.)*

2. Our Father (Lord's Prayer)

Our Father, who art in heaven, hallowed be thy name; thy kingdom come; thy will be done on earth as it is in heaven. Give us this day our daily bread; and forgive us our trespasses as we forgive those who trespass against us; and lead us not into temptation, but deliver us from evil.

3. Hail Mary

Hail Mary, full of grace. The Lord is with thee. Blessed art thou amongst women, and blessed is the fruit of thy womb, Jesus. Holy Mary, Mother of God, pray for us sinners, now and at the hour of our death. Amen.

4. Prayer of Praise (Glory Be)

Glory be to the Father, and to the Son, and to the Holy Spirit, as it was in the beginning, is now, and ever shall be, world without end. Amen.

5. Apostles' Creed

I believe in God, the Father almighty, creator of heaven and earth; and in Jesus Christ, his only Son, our Lord; who was conceived by the Holy Spirit, born of the virgin Mary, suffered under Pontius Pilate, was crucified, died, and was buried. He descended to the dead; the third day he arose again from the dead; he ascended into heaven, sits at the right hand of God, the Father almighty; from thence he shall come to judge the living and the dead. I believe in the Holy Spirit, the Holy Catholic Church, the communion of saints, the forgiveness of sins, the resurrection of the body, and life everlasting. Amen.

6. A Morning Prayer
(Canticle of Zechariah — Luke 1:68-79)

Blessed be the Lord God of Israel,
for he has visited and redeemed his people,
and has raised up a horn of salvation for us
in the house of his servant David,
as he spoke by the mouth of his holy prophets from of old,
that we should be saved from our enemies,
and from the hand of all who hate us;
to perform the mercy promised to our father,
and to remember his holy covenant,

the oath which he swore to our father Abraham
to grant us that we,
being delivered from the hand of our enemies,
might serve him without fear,
in holiness and righteousness before him
all the days of our life.
And you, child, will be called the prophet
of the Most High;
for you will go before the Lord to prepare his ways,
to give knowledge of salvation to his people
in the forgiveness of their sins,
through the tender mercy of our God,
when the day shall dawn upon us from on high
to give light to those who sit in darkness
and in the shadow of death,
to guide our feet into the way of peace.

7. Morning Offering

Almighty God, we thank you for your past blessings. Today, we offer ourselves, our family — whatever we do, say, or think — to your loving care. Continue to bless us, Lord.

We make this morning offering in union with the divine intentions of Jesus Christ who offers himself daily in the holy Sacrifice of the Mass, and in union with Mary, his Virgin Mother and our Mother, who was always the faithful handmaid of the Lord.

8. A Morning Prayer (Romans 8:35-39)

Who will separate us from the love of Christ? Trial, or distress, or persecution, or hunger, or nakedness, or danger or the sword? As Scripture says: "For your sake we are being slain all the day long; we are looked upon as sheep to be slaughtered." Yet in all this we are more than conquerors because of him who has loved us. For I am certain that neither death nor life, neither angels nor principalities, neither the present nor the future, nor powers, neither height nor depth nor any other creature, will be able to separate us from the love of God that comes to us in Christ Jesus, our Lord.

9. Noonday Prayer (Angelus)

The angel of the Lord declared unto Mary.
Response: And she conceived of the Holy Spirit. (Hail Mary)
Behold the handmaid of the Lord.
Response: May it be done unto me according to your word. (Hail Mary)
And the Word was made flesh.
Response: And dwelt among us. (Hail Mary)
Pray for us, O Holy Mother of God.
Response: That we may be made worthy of the promises of Christ.

Let us pray. O Lord, it was through the message of an angel that we learned of the incarnation of Christ, your Son. Pour your grace into our hearts, and by his Passion and Cross bring us to the glory of his Resurrection. Through Christ, our Lord. Amen.

10. Noonday Prayer (at Eastertime instead of Angelus)

Queen of heaven, rejoice, Alleluia.
Response: The Son whom you were privileged to bear, Alleluia, has risen as he said, Alleluia.
Pray to God for us, Alleluia. Rejoice and be glad, Virgin Mary, Alleluia.
Response: For the Lord has truly risen, Alleluia.

Let us pray. O God, it was by the Resurrection of your Son, our Lord Jesus Christ, that you brought joy to the world. Grant that through the intercession of the Virgin Mary, his Mother, we may attain the joy of eternal life. Through Christ, our Lord. Amen.

11. Prayer before Meals

From the heavens he sends down rain and rich harvests; our spirits he fills with food and delight.

Bless us, O Lord, and these your gifts, which we are about to receive from your goodness, through Christ, our Lord.

May the Lord provide for the needs of others and always be our heavenly food. Amen.

12. Prayer after Meals

We give you thanks, almighty God, for all your gifts and favors: who live and reign forever.
Response: Amen.
May the king of everlasting glory make us partakers at the heavenly table.
Response: May he lead us to the banquet of eternal life.
In your mercy, Lord, grant everlasting life to all who have been generous toward us for your sake.
Response: Glory be to the Father, and to the Son, and to the Holy Spirit, as it was in the beginning, is now, and ever shall be, world without end. Amen.

(It is also good to pray spontaneously, especially before meals. Begin with a short passage from sacred Scripture, then pray silently or aloud in your own words. Let each member focus on your family oneness with Jesus in the Eucharist by saying silently: Because there is one bread, we who are many are one body, for we all partake of the one bread.)

13. Evening Examination of Conscience (1 Cor 13:4-7)

(Pause for a few seconds after each phrase so that all can recall their loving and unloving acts of the day. Afterward, let each person thank God for the grace of having loved, and ask his grace to seek forgiveness of anyone offended.)

Love is patient and kind; / love is not jealous or boastful; / it is not arrogant or rude. / Love does not insist on its own way; / it is not irritable or resentful; / it does not rejoice at wrong, but rejoices in the right. / Love bears all things, / believes all things, / hopes all things, / endures all things.

14. Act of Contrition

My God, I am sorry for my sins with all my heart. In choosing to do wrong and failing to do good, I have sinned against you whom I should love above all things. I firmly intend, with your help, to do penance, to sin no more, and to avoid whatever leads me to sin. Our Savior Jesus Christ suffered and died for us. In his name, my God, have mercy.

15. Evening Prayer (Canticle of Mary — Luke 1:46-55)

My soul magnifies the Lord,
and my spirit rejoices in God my Savior,
for he has regarded the low estate of his handmaiden.
For behold, henceforth all generations
will call me blessed;
for he who is mighty has done great things for me,
and holy is his name.
And his mercy is on those who fear him
from generation to generation.
He has shown strength with his arm,
he has scattered the proud
in the imagination of their hearts,
he has put down the mighty from their thrones,
and exalted those of low degree;
he has filled the hungry with good things,
and the rich he has sent empty away.
He has helped his servant Israel,
in remembrance of his mercy,
as he spoke to our fathers,
to Abraham and to his posterity forever.

16. The Family Rosary

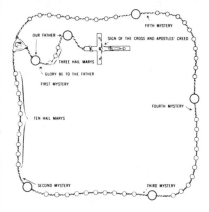

HOW TO PRAY THE ROSARY

The complete rosary is composed of fifteen decades, but it is divided into three distinct parts, each containing five decades. The first part consists of five joyful events (called *mysteries*) in the life of Jesus and Mary. The second part recalls five sorrowful events, and the third part recalls five glorious events.

Begin the rosary by making the sign of the cross. Then say the Apostles' Creed, one Our Father, three Hail Marys, and one Glory Be to the Father on the small chain. (When praying the rosary as a family, the person leading it says the first part of each prayer aloud, and the others respond by saying aloud the second part — for example, "Holy Mary, Mother of God . . . .")

Now recall the first mystery (Joyful, Sorrowful, or Glorious) you are praying, and on the beads for the first decade say one Our Father, ten Hail Marys, and one Glory Be to the Father. The other decades are said in the same way, recalling the other events or mysteries you are praying. Like any other prayer, the rosary is good for your family only if it helps you to be in touch with God. Some families find that one decade of the rosary each evening, rather than five decades, is better for their spirit of prayer.

At the end of the rosary, there is a custom of reciting the Hail, Holy Queen.

The rosary is a Biblical and traditional Catholic prayer that is especially suited to our modern age. As Pope Paul VI pointed out, the rosary has been called "the compendium of the entire

Gospel." The repetition of the Hail Mary, if you let it, can put your mind in a state of calm attention to the divine Mystery present in your midst. In this connection, Pope Paul noted that without this element of contemplation, the rosary "is a body without a soul, and its recitation is in danger of becoming a mechanical repetition of formulas" (*Marialis Cultus* 47; see Matthew 6:7).

The Joyful Mysteries

1. The messenger of God announces to Mary that she is to be the Mother of God. (After each mystery, a virtue is presented for practical application in your family life. The virtue for this mystery is *Humility.*)
2. Mary visits and helps her cousin Elizabeth. (*Love of Neighbor*)
3. Mary gives birth to Jesus in a stable of Bethlehem. (*Spirit of Poverty*)
4. Jesus is presented in the Temple. (*Obedience to God's Will*)
5. Jesus is found in the Temple. (*Fidelity to Vocation*)

The Sorrowful Mysteries

1. Jesus undergoes his agony in the Garden of Gethsemane. (*Spirit of Prayer*)
2. Jesus is scourged at the pillar. (*Modesty and Purity*)
3. Jesus is crowned with thorns. (*Courage*)
4. Jesus carries the cross to Calvary. (*Patience in Suffering*)
5. Jesus dies on the cross for our sins. (*Self-denial*)

The Glorious Mysteries

1. Jesus rises from the dead. (*Faith*)
2. Jesus ascends into heaven. (*Hope*)
3. The Holy Spirit comes to the apostles and the Blessed Mother. (*Wisdom, Love, Zeal, Fortitude*)
4. The Mother of Jesus is taken into heaven. (*Anticipation of Eternal Happiness*)
5. Mary is crowned queen of heaven and earth. (*Devotion to (Mary and Final Perseverance*)

17. Hail, Holy Queen

Hail, Holy Queen, mother of mercy, our life, our sweetness, and our hope. To you we cry, poor banished children of Eve; to you we send up our sighs, mourning and weeping in this valley of tears. Turn then, O most gracious advocate, your eyes of mercy toward us, and after this our exile, show unto us the blessed fruit of your womb, Jesus. O clement, O loving, O sweet virgin Mary.

Pray for us, O holy Mother of God.

Response: That we may be made worthy of the promises of Christ.

Let us pray. O God, whose only begotten Son, by his life, death, and Resurrection, has purchased for us the rewards of eternal life, grant, we beseech you, that meditating upon these mysteries of the most holy rosary of the Blessed Virgin Mary, we may imitate what they contain and obtain what they promise. Through the same Christ our Lord. Amen.

18. Prayer for the One Human Family

O Father, Mystery at the heart of our lives, you have told us through the Second Vatican Council that "here grows the body of a new human family, a body which even now is able to give some kind of foreshadowing of the new age."

Make us convinced that after we have "nurtured on earth the values of human dignity, brotherhood and freedom, and indeed all the good fruits of our nature and enterprise, we will find them again, but freed of stain, burnished and transfigured . . . .

Let us see that the day has already begun when you "will wipe away every tear from our eyes, and death shall be no more"; that the day has already begun when you say to all living things: "Behold, I make all things new . . . . It is done! I am the Alpha and the Omega, the Beginning and the End."

Meanwhile, with the early Christians, we cry out: *Marana tha!* Come, Lord Jesus! We seek you.

SECTION THREE: CATHOLIC FAMILY RESOURCES

Printed Materials and Cassette Tapes

Please order any of the materials listed here from your local religious bookstore or from their publishers.

If you order materials published by Liguori Publications, please add 50¢ for postage and handling. Write or call: Liguori Publications, One Liguori Drive, Liguori, MO 63057. Phone (314) 464-2500.

- *Redeemer of Man* is the first encyclical letter of Pope John Paul II. Traditional in the genuine sense, and also prophetic, the encyclical centers on Christ, and the unity of the Church's mission with the promoting of human dignity, which is rooted in the Gospel message. To order, write or call: Publications Office, United States Catholic Conference, 1312 Massachusetts Avenue, N.W., Washington, D.C. 20005. Phone: (202) 659-6640. (Cost: $1.50)

- The USCC Commission on Marriage and Family Life offers several resources for implementing the Bishops' Plan of Pastoral Action for Family Ministry.

  For diocesan planners, *Sounds of the Family,* 120 pages, is "A Pastoral Listening and Planning Workbook" designed to facilitate the Action Plan process (cost: $12.50).

  For parishes and families, *A Vision and a Strategy,* 48 pages illustrated, contains the Plan, a discussion guide for home and parish, and selected Church documentation (cost: $1.75). A *Ministry Resource Packet,* for parishes and families, contains one copy each of: *A Vision and a Strategy; Models of Ministry* (resource examples for parish-family ministry); *Households of Faith* (for families); *Parish Planning Calendar* (including a booklet helpful to families planning events and parish conversations (cost: $7.50).

  The following audio-visual materials are also available: *Sounds of the Family,* a 12-minute/20-second filmstrip and cassette (cost: $25); an audio-cassette by Dr. David M. Thomas, "Pastoral Approach to Family Ministry"/"Family Spirituality" (cost: $5); *Planning for Family Ministry,* a filmstrip about the Pastoral Action Plan (cost: $25). These three items are available in an A-V kit for home, neighborhood, and parish use for $45. Write or call: USCC Office of Creative Services, 1312 Massachusetts Avenue, N.W., Washington, D.C. 20005. Phone: (202) 659-6754.

- In 64 pages, the *Handbook for Today's Catholic: Beliefs – Practices – Prayers* presents basic beliefs, drawing mainly from Vatican II, "the great catechism of our times" (Pope Paul VI); basic practices that believing Catholics perform; basic prayers used by Catholics in their heart-to-heart relationship with God. A $1 booklet from Liguori Publications.

- The Xavier Society for the Blind offers a free 14-page weekly newsletter to the deaf-blind, entitled *Deafblind Weekly*. The newsletter includes Church and world news in Braille and on tape.

  XSB also offers a free monthly Braille magazine, the *Catholic Review*, in Braille, on cassette tape, and in large print. The *Liguorian* magazine is available in these three forms. Also available in Braille and in large print are the Sunday Mass readings.

  Also available from XSB is a catalog of taped books — spiritual and leisure reading, Catholic magazines, the Bible, etc. For a copy of this catalog, and for the newsletter and magazine noted above, write: Xavier Society for the Blind, 154 E. 23rd Street, New York, NY 10010.

- A family-oriented information packet for parents, teachers, and others, from The Christophers, includes six *Christopher News Notes* on marriage, family, children, aging, communication, listening/friendship. The *Notes* on family communication describe common faults causing lack of communication and suggest ways to communicate effectively. Single packets are available free.

  "Choosing Life — Some Questions and Answers on Abortion" is the title of another excellent, free *News Note*. Also available for an offering of $3.50 is a 28-minute tape cassette entitled *Alternative to Abortion*. For all of the above, write: The Christophers, 12 E. 48th Street, New York, NY 10010.

- *Closed Marriage: Almost Always You Marry the Right Person* is a book that counters the "anti-marriage brainwashing" trend. Author Herbert A. Glieberman, married over 20 years, is "the divorce lawyer who tries to save marriages."

Treating topics such as religion, changes in life-style, commitment, drinking, and money problems, the book helps cut difficulties down to size. Published by Sheed Andrews and McMeel, Inc., 6700 Squibb Road, Mission, KS 66202.

• Practical books, booklets, and pamphlets on Catholic marriage and family life are available from Liguori Publications. Titles include:

Your Marriage, by John F. DeYonker, D.O. and Thomas E. Tobin, C.SS.R. Paperback, $1.50.

Living and Loving: A Guide to a Happy Marriage, by Gordon Lester, C.SS.R. Paperback, $1.75.

Hurrah for Parents!, by Charles A. Gallagher, S.J. Paperback, $2.95.

Will Religion Make Sense to Your Child?, by Earnest Larsen and Patricia Galvin. Paperback, $1.95.

Helping Your Child Know Right from Wrong, A Redemptorist Pastoral Publication. Paperback, $2.50.

The Six Levels of a Happy Marriage, by Rev. Medard Laz. A $1 booklet.

The 9 Most Common Marriage Problems and How to Overcome Them, by James J. Rue, Ph.D. A $1 booklet.

Coping with Widowhood, by Frances Caldwell Durland. A $1 booklet.

For a free catalog of books and/or pamphlets (including pamphlets in Spanish) write or call: Liguori Publications, One Liguori Drive, Liguori, MO 63057. Phone: (314) 464-2500.

• *Sexual Morality: Guidelines for Today's Catholic* (formerly *Sex Sanity in the Modern World),* by Fr. Russell Abata, C.SS.R., covers the range of human sexual life from the viewpoint of an experienced priest-counselor who is trained in moral theology. A $1 booklet from Liguori Publications.

- Two excellent works that offer realistic guidance and help with problems of alcoholism are:

    Alcohol and the Family: Three Sure Ways to Solve the Problem, by Father Frank, C.SS.R. This booklet explains why Alcoholics Anonymous and (organizations for family members) Al-Anon and Alateen are successful. A $1 booklet from Liguori Publications.

    "I'm not an alcoholic because . . .", by Richard L. Reilly, D.O. From his experience in rehabilitating over 7,000 persons, Dr. Reilly offers a candid, descriptive explanation of the excuses/reasons people give for their drinking problems. A paperback book from Liguori Publications, $2.95.

- For separated and divorced and/or remarried Catholics, there is a group that builds mutual support and healing. Known as NACSDC (North American Conference of Separated and Divorced Catholics), the group creates a sense of belonging within the Church community. Information can be obtained from: NACSDC, 5 Park Street, Boston, MA 02108. Phone: (617) 742-4462.

    The Pain and the Possibility: Divorce and Separation Among Catholics is a book by Sister Paula Ripple, executive director of NACSDC. The book offers support and encouragement to divorced and separated people and also to their parents, relatives, and friends. Published by: Ave Maria Press, Notre Dame, IN 46556. Phone: (219) 283-7208.

- *Successful Single Parenting* (formerly *A Parent Alone*), by Antoinette Bosco, is the informative story of a woman who survived the trauma of divorce and reared her six children alone. The book contains advice for all parents — especially single parents — stressing the joy of family oneness. A paperback book from Twenty-Third Publications, P.O. Box 180, West Mystic, CT 06388.

- A leading Catholic magazine for families is the *Liguorian,* published by the Redemptorist Fathers. Practical and timely, the *Liguorian* enters nearly a half million homes monthly. Subscription rates are: one year, $5; three years, $10; five years, $15. (Add $1 for subscriptions to Canada and other countries.) Write or call: *Liguorian,* One Liguori Drive, Liguori, MO 63057. Phone: (314) 464-2500.

- In each monthly issue, *Marriage and Family Living* magazine publishes a section called "Family Night," which offers ideas for weekly activities, family sharing and entertainment, and prayer. Write or call: Subscription Service, Marriage, St. Meinrad, IN 47577. Phone: (812) 357-8251.

- Two very informative and practical booklets for family Scripture are:
  How to Read and Pray the Gospels, by Marilyn Norquist.
  How to Read and Pray Saint Paul, by Marilyn Norquist.
  Both booklets contain practical "Suggestions for Family Use" in each chapter. The booklet on the letters of Saint Paul also contains a wealth of Paul's advice for Catholics *as parishioners.* Both are $1.50 booklets from Liguori Publications.

- A cassette tape entitled *Reading and Praying the Scriptures – A Practical Approach,* by Fr. William Meninger, O.C.S.O., who developed the centering prayer method, is available from The Abbey Gift Shop, Spencer, MA 01562.

- Two excellent books which explain the concept and practice of centering prayer are:
  Finding Grace at the Center, by Trappists Thomas Keating and M. Basil Pennington, and Thomas E. Clarke, S.J. A list of

sources at the back of the book includes addresses of places in the United States where workshops on centering prayer are offered. A paperback book from St. Bede Publications, Still River, MA 01467. Phone: (617) 456-8574.

Daily We Touch Him, by M. Basil Pennington, O.C.S.O. An Image paperback book from Doubleday & Company, Inc., 245 Park Avenue, New York, NY 10017.

The 14th-century spiritual classic, *The Cloud of Unknowing,* from which centering prayer is derived, is available in a modern edition, with a superb Introduction, by William Johnston, S.J. An Image paperback book from Doubleday & Company, Inc., 245 Park Avenue, New York, NY 10017.

● A beautiful book, *Morning and Evening Prayer,* contains selections from the Liturgy of the Hours for morning and evening, edited for popular use by Rev. D. Joseph Finnerty and Rev. George J. Ryan. (No longer restricted to religious and clergy, the Liturgy of the Hours is now the prayer of all Christians.) Ideal for couples who wish to pray together at the start and end of the day. The various sections of the book cover the Church year and each day of the week, including prayers in honor of the Blessed Virgin Mary and prayers for the dead. Published by Regina Press, 7 Midland Avenue, Hicksville, NY 11801. Phone: (516) 681-7474.

● *Advent Begins at Home: Family Prayers and Activities,* by David Polek, C.SS.R., and Rita Anderhub, is designed to help families share the true meaning of Advent and Christmas. The illustrated booklet includes an Advent calendar with daily suggestions for discussion, Bible readings, prayers, and practices. A $1 booklet from Liguori Publications.

Lent Begins at Home: Family Prayers and Activities, by Pat and Rosemary Ryan, a companion to *Advent Begins at Home,* includes a Lenten calendar with daily suggestions for family discussions, Bible readings, prayers, and practices. A $1.50 booklet from Liguori Publications.

- *Church: Sign of God's Kingdom,* by Fr. John McPhee, describes a form of parish community-in-dialogue based on the experience of thousands of Catholics in the United States. Called Christian communions, clusters of 10 to 15 families work together with the priests and religious of the parish to revitalize Christian life in the neighborhood. To order, write or call: St. Norbert's Parish, 604 Sherbourne Drive, Inkster, MI 48141. Phone: (313) 563-0993.

- *Operation Homecoming* is the name of a tested parish program that invites non-practicing Catholics back home. The program is relatively simple, works well, and parishioners have a strong role in it. It has proven highly rewarding both to the evangelizers and to those evangelized. For a packet containing materials used, plus reports based on two years of experience, write or call: Fr. Daniel J. O'Connor, Pastor, St. Thomas Aquinas Church, 535 Rucker Road, Alpharetta, GA 30201. Phone: (404) 475-4501. (Cost: $5.00)

- A practical study booklet to help parish leaders plan parish education programs on human rights and peace is entitled *Human Rights/Human Needs – An Unfinished Agenda.* The booklet tells how parishes can promote human rights at the local, national, and international levels. It includes Church and United Nations documentation, a resource list, and activity suggestions. Write or call: USCC Justice and Peace Office, 1312 Massachusetts Avenue, N.W., Washington, D.C. 20005. Phone: (202) 659-6820. (Copies are 75¢ each, prepaid; bulk discounts.)

- *Poverty: Who Needs It,* by Fr. David Knight, a poverty expert, is a Gospel call to a simple life-style, offering action principles for laypeople, religious, and priests. 20 pages, 8½ x 11. Write: CRUX, 75 Champlain Street, Albany, NY 12204. (Cost: $1.55, including postage; bulk rates available for parish study groups, etc.)

- For parish leaders, an outstanding weekly newsletter for information on Catholic resources is *CRUX of the News*. Rates are $24.75 (U.S. currency) for one year, $44.25 for two years.

  Also available is an excellent *monthly* newsletter, *The Crux of PRAYER,* designed to help deepen personal prayer life, communal prayer, and efforts in developing prayer activity among others. $15.75 per year. For a subscription to either or both newsletters, write or call: CRUX, 75 Champlain Street, Albany, NY 12204. Phone: (518) 434-2616.

Organizations and Movements

- The *Focolare Movement,* started in Italy in 1943, is a Catholic organization with centers in some 150 countries. Basic core-group members have vows and live in separate men's and women's communities. Groups include families, youth, seminarians, religious, priests. FM provides mutual spiritual support and works toward Church unity. Focolare publishes a bi-monthly magazine, *Living City,* as well as a series of books on family life. For information and/or a catalog of publications, write or call: Focolare Movement, P.O. Box 496, New York, NY 10021. Phone (212) 249-8283 (Women's National Director in the United States) *or* (212) 387-3454 (Men's National Director in the United States).

- Begun by Catholic couples and priests in the 1940s, the *Christian Family Movement* (CFM) is ecumenical, encouraging Protestant and inter-faith groups. The goal of CFM is "the development of couples, their families and others in their personal relationships through social consciousness and involvement.'' For a free information kit, write or call: Christian Family Movement, National Office, 2500 New York Avenue, P.O. Box 792, Whiting, IN 46394. Phone: (219) 659-0150.

- The largest pro-marriage group in the world is *Worldwide Marriage Encounter*. After ME weekends, the aim of which is to make good marriages better, members keep in touch. For information on WWME in your area, write: 3711 Long Beach Blvd., Suite 204, Long Beach, CA 90807. Phone: (213) 595-5336.

  National Marriage Encounter is a separate organization with its own distinctive emphases. Write: National Marriage Encounter, 955 Lake Drive, St. Paul, MN 55120. Phone: (612) 454-6437.

- *Engaged Encounter* is a weekend experience, directed by two married Catholic couples and a priest, designed to help engaged couples to dialogue intensively about their prospective lives together. Interested couples can inquire at their diocesan Family Life Bureau. If there is no Engaged Encounter available in the diocese, write: Engaged Encounter, c/o Pete and Barbara Inglese, 34 Fishhawk Drive, Middletown, NJ 17748, for locations and dates.

- *The Parish Renewal Weekend*, developed by Fr. Charles A. Gallagher, S.J., is a dynamic experience in Catholic identity, evangelization, and parish renewal. Open to laypeople, priests, and religious, weekends are held in numerous locations in the United States and abroad. For locations and dates, write or call: Parish Renewal Weekend, 567 Morris Avenue, Elizabeth, NJ 07208. Phone: (201) 353-8640.

- The Committee for Pro-Life Activities, of the United States National Conference of Catholic Bishops (NCCB), has a catalog of its publications. Write or call: Committee for Pro-Life Activities, NCCB, 1312 Massachusetts Avenue, N.W., Washington, D.C. 20005. Phone: (202) 659-6673.

- Experience and research show undesirable effects from artificial birth control and good effects from two modern methods of natural family planning: the ovulation method, and the sympto-thermal method. These two advanced methods allow couples to insure conception, when desired, as well as to avoid conception safely when it is not desired. Not least among the experienced benefits of NFP is greater family closeness.

The Couple to Couple League (CCL) is an organization devoted to giving first-rate training in NFP to married couples. All over the United States, hundreds of certified couples teach other couples the full sympto-thermal method of NFP, as well as ecological breast-feeding, in a way that supports Catholic religious values. Write or call: The Couple to Couple League, P.O. Box 11084, Cincinnati, OH 45211. Phone: (513) 661-7612.

Two closely linked organizations which promote the sympto-thermal and the ovulation methods of NFP, and which publish materials for interested couples, are:

The Human Life Center, Rev. Paul Marx, O.S.B., Executive Director, St. John's University, Collegeville, MN 56321. Phone: (612) 363-3552 and 363-3313.

The Family Life Association, Rev. Anthony Zimmerman, S.V.D., Executive Director, Yuwa Building, Shiba 3-4-16, Minatoku, Tokyo, Japan.